WHAT DOES JESUS HATE?

(The Deeds of the Nicolaitans- Rev.2)

ROBERT S HERNDON

WHAT DOES JESUS HATE?
(The Deeds of the Nicolaitans- Rev.2)
by Robert S Herndon

Printed in the United States of America.

ISBN 9781498478359

www.xulonpress.com

TABLE OF CONTENTS

ACKNOWLEDGEMENTS

I would like to thank my friend and mentor, Dr. J.T. Parish, whom I had the privilege of working with in ministry for several years. While I was his youth pastor at Christian Fellowship Church in Kentucky, Bro. Parish provided me with a vast amount of Bible knowledge and inspiration by living the Christian example in true humility and love, showing me that one can truly be a man of God in this world today. He, being an author of several books, gave me the nudge I needed to publish this book and I am more than honored.

I would also like to acknowledge my friend, Brother Harold Witmer, Pastor of Community Church in Clarksville, Tennessee. Harold founded many different ministries over the years, ministering to soldiers, young people, and on the mission field in Russia. He has individually led more people to Christ than anyone I know. After reading his autobiography, *Brother Harold,* I was inspired to go through with the writing and publishing of this book.

I would also like to remember my great-uncle, Dr. H. Thornton Fowler who served as a pastor, evangelist, District Superintendent, and director of the United Methodist Publishing House in Nashville. I remember him for his inspiration and encouragement when I first felt the call to the ministry. He also warned me of some of the things I will be discussing in this book.

Most of all, I would like to thank Jesus for giving me the ability to live and move and have my being…and write this book.

FOREWORD

I t is obvious that the Body of Christ, AKA the Church, is not as effective today as it could be. You have heard it said that 20% of the people do 80% of the work. I believe in most cases, it is closer to 10% (and that is not what the Bible means by "tithing"). What if that trend was reversed? When Jesus warned the Church about the doctrines and deeds of the Nicolaitans in Revelation 2, He hated the effect that it would have on his Body as if it were an infection or disease that would debilitate it. The secret to curing a disease is, first, identifying it. Then the Doctor can administer the cure. When you read this book, you will see how widespread this doctrine has infiltrated the Church.

In Revelation 2 and 3, Jesus told us what was right and wrong with the seven churches of Asia. I believe that all of these admonitions speak to the Universal Church today. The good news is, Jesus also offered the cure. It was one word, "repent". The admonition to repent can be applied to the doctrines and deeds of the Nicolaitans, and when it does, we will see a work of God that has never before taken place upon the earth. We will see the 10% become the 90% or better. We will see a great revival.

INTRODUCTION

Revelation 2:6 "But this you have, that you hate the deeds of the **Nicolaitans**, **which I also hate."**

Revelation 2:15 "Thus you also have those who hold the doctrine of the **Nicolaitans**, **which thing I hate."**

How many times have you read these words and skimmed over them? Maybe you scratched your head and thought, "what does that mean"? Maybe you took out a Bible commentary and looked up their explanation, if you could find it, but it did not seem to satisfy your curiosity. Furthermore, how many times have we heard Jesus say that He *hated* something? More interestingly, He said it after the resurrection and ascension into Heaven. If Jesus is addressing the Church with language He has never used before, it is time to listen to what He is saying.

In this book, we are going to find out what that warning means and discover how this thing that Jesus hates has affected the course of history in the Church and the Church today. We will find that the doctrines and works of the Nicolaitans have adversely influenced and hindered the work and purpose of the Church since the early days.

The good news is, there is still time to recognize and fix it today. In fact, this notion is backed by Bible prophecy of a great awakening before Jesus returns. This will only come about when everyone in the Body of Christ recognizes that God has a purpose and calling for each individual and that each one is as important as the other.

I realize that this book is opening a "can of worms", and many will reject this idea. However, the Holy Spirit put this seed in my mind around 1979 and it kept growing. Many times, I try to ignore it, "prune it", and constantly procrastinate, but the more I studied and prayed about it, the more I realized that I had to write this book.

I am asking each reader to look at this book from a completely scriptural perspective. Over the years, there has been much theology applied to this subject that has tried to excuse it, but it never complies with the ultimate test, the Bible. You will find that the doctrines and works of the Nicolaitans have contradicted and worked against the Scriptures. Many of the things that we do in the Church are created by man without the leadership of the Holy

Spirit and they hinder and cause harm rather than good.

The other thing I am asking you to do is to pray and ask the Holy Spirit to confirm this in your heart. Some of you will say, "yes, this is what I have felt in my heart, but I didn't know how to put it in words!" Others will say, "this guy is a heretic and needs to be burned at the stake!" All I can ask you to do is to open your hearts and pray.

Chapter 1

WHAT IS A NICOLAITAN?

When we think of Jesus, we think of **love.** "Jesus loves me this I know, for the Bible tells me so…" comes to mind with an image of Jesus holding a child in his lap and maybe some sheep in the background. This is good. This is an image of what Jesus feels for us, his children and it exemplifies the fact that He is the Great Shepherd and has the ultimate heart of a shepherd. What we have to remember though, is that a shepherd loves and protects his sheep.

Jesus is the epitome of love and He even taught us to love our enemies and pray for those who despitefully use us. On the cross, some of his last words were, "Father, forgive them, they know not what they do…".

Albeit, when Jesus is speaking to the seven churches in Revelation, chapters two and three, what does He mean when He says, "But this you have, that you hate the deeds of the **Nicolaitans**, which I also **hate**" (Rev. 2:6), and "Thus you also have those who hold the doctrine of the **Nicolaitans**, which thing I **hate**"? (Rev. 2:15). Jesus is correcting, admonishing, edifying, exhorting, and comforting his sheep. Another thing He is doing is warning the sheep to beware of the wolves (false teaching was the potential downfall of the churches of Thyatira and Pergamos). In Matthew 17:15, Jesus said, **Beware of false prophets, who come to you in sheep's clothing, but inwardly they are ravenous wolves**. The "elephant in the room" is, what could be important enough to Jesus that would cause Him to say that He *hates* it

16

when He is addressing the Seven Churches of Asia (which I believe represents all of the churches throughout history including today)?

WHAT DOES THE WORD, NICOLAITAN MEAN?

The next obvious question should be, what is a *Nicolaitan*?

If you go by what several commentaries say, you will find that they say a Nicolaitan is a follower of a first-century heretic named *Nicolas*. Most commentaries will precede that with the disclaimer, "many scholars believe...". During the time of the early Church, there were many false teachers and heretics already active. Two examples were found in Acts 5:34⁻

Then one in the council stood up, a Pharisee named Gamaliel, a teacher of the law held in respect by all the people, and commanded them to put the apostles outside for a little while. ³⁵ And he said to them: "Men of Israel, take heed to yourselves what you intend to do regarding these men. ³⁶ For some time ago Theudas rose up, claiming to be somebody. A number of men, about four hundred, joined him. He was slain, and all who obeyed him were scattered and came to nothing. ³⁷ After this man, Judas of Galilee rose up in the days of the census, and drew away many people after him. He also perished, and all who obeyed him were dispersed. ³⁸ And now I say to you, keep away from these men and let them alone; **for if this plan or this work is of men, it will come to nothing; ³⁹ but if it is of God, you**

*cannot overthrow it—lest you even
be found to fight against God.*

Gamaliel's advice was good and wise. That being the case, why was Jesus so concerned about another heretic named Nicolas? **I do not believe that this is what Jesus was saying.** He was not talking about an isolated false teacher. He was talking about a doctrine that Satan was sowing like seeds among the churches. This means that the word, *Nicolaitan*, means something far more significant and sinister. This was first brought to my attention when I was reading a verse-by-verse commentary or Bible study on Revelation written by pastor Chuck Smith back in the '70s, called *What the World Is Coming To*. He commented on Rev. 2:6-7 and said, "'Nicolaitans' comes from two Greek words: *nikao* and *laos* meaning 'establishing a priesthood over laity.' The church of Ephesus hated that establishment of a spiritual hierarchy. Jesus said, 'Which I also hate.' Why? Because, in our minds, it suddenly puts some men closer to God than others." [1]

In Matthew 27:50-51, it says, *And Jesus cried out again with a loud voice, and yielded up His spirit. 51 Then, behold, the veil of the temple was torn in two from top to bottom; and the earth quaked, and the rocks were split.* When Jesus died on the cross, the Veil of the Temple that separated us from the Holy of Holies was torn in two. Jesus opened the way for all of us to have equal access to all of the glory of God that the High Priest had in the Old Covenant. I Timothy 2:5-6 says, **For there is one God and one Mediator between God and men, the Man Christ Jesus, who gave Himself a ransom for all, to be testified in due**

---

[1] Chuck Smith, *What the World is Coming To,* The Word for Today 2006. Costa Mesa, CA, p. 22.

time.[2] The teachings of the Nicolaitans went back to the Old Covenant and even farther to maintain the practice of having another person stand in the place of God and be the mediator. With the New Covenant, Jesus became the mediator for all of us to have direct access to God the Father. I consider it blasphemy for another human being to try to usurp that place which Jesus himself stands. If there was another human being who was born of a virgin with God as his bio-logical father, who spent a lifetime teaching Truth directly from Heaven, who worked mir-acles, who never sinned, who was crucified and took the blame and punishment for all of our sins, who descended into the bowels of the earth and rose after three days, who ascended into Heaven and now sits at the right hand of God the Father, and who is

---

[2] Scripture references will be from the New King James Bible unless otherwise noted.

coming back again to judge and reign; then he might be able to qualify as another Mediator. I'm pretty sure no one else meets those qualifications.

Yet, we see the church today in most denominations and many "non-denominations" doing that very thing. We see people called "clergy" (an unscriptural term) separated from laity (another unscriptural term) exercising authority to perform ceremonies, rituals, and sacraments (yet another unbiblical term for the New Testament) that your lowly "laypeople" cannot perform.

What does the Scripture say about this?

2 Corinthians 5 says: **18** *Now all things are of God, who has reconciled us to Himself through Jesus Christ, and has given us the ministry of reconciliation, 19 that is, that God was in Christ reconciling the world to Himself, not imputing*

their trespasses to them, and has committed to us the word of reconciliation.

20 Now then, we are ambassadors for Christ, as though God were pleading through us: we implore you on Christ's behalf, be reconciled to God. 21 For He made Him who knew no sin to be sin for us, that we might become the righteousness of God in Him.

When the veil was torn in two, Jesus opened the doors of the Kingdom of God to whoever would meet one qualification; **to believe**! *Then, …He ascended on high, He led captivity captive, And **gave gifts to men**.* (Ephesians 4:8). Martin Luther called it "the priesthood of the believer". God gave all of us gifts to qualify us to be ministers with our own individual traits and characteristics to enable us to reach people that might not be reached through anyone else. We are not supposed to sit in a pew or folding chair and watch the "professional" ministers preach, sing, and perform. We are not to go about our own daily business while we know that the clergy does our good deeds, visitation and benevolent service for us. We are all called to go into the world and make disciples. **The reason the church is on the decline is because we are depending upon a "chosen few" to do our work for us due to this false doctrine.** I believe that one reason Jesus hated this doctrine was because the work of spreading the Gospel would not get done.

The doctrine of the Nicolaitans reinforces the statement that Jesus made when He said, "The harvest truly is plentiful, but the **laborers are few"**. It "disqualifies" people who are already qualified.

In the seminaries of the mainstream denominations, there is a strong emphasis on separation of clergy and laity. I was in a conference among ministers in recent years and keynote speaker was a seminary professor. She was addressing the relationship between clergy and laity and looked up and said in a dreamy sort of voice, "…you will never be one of them." My first thought was, "newsflash lady, we always were." We are all flesh that is like grass that withers away. We are housings for our spirits that, through believing, join with His Spirit and become vessels of God. A few seminary classes do not make us more qualified to be God's vessels. In fact, the false teachings of the "higher criticism" that have crept into most seminaries have had the opposite effect and allowed unbelief to permeate much of the preaching and teaching in the pulpits today. The average "lay-person" is taken in by these teachings and believes them because the "professional" has used that position of authority to impose it upon them. After all, who are "laity" to question those in authority? In John 9, the "professional" clergy of the day were asking that same question while looking for a reason to accuse Jesus. Because He had made a clay paste with his saliva and put on the blind man's eyes, the Pharisees were eager to accuse Jesus of breaking the Sabbath. Their envy and jealousy blinded them to the truth. Their feeling of power and control was threatened to the point that they ignored the fact that a man who had been blind from birth was now seeing. These Nicolaitans were actually the ones who were blind while the "layperson" could see.

I would answer that question ("Who are laity to question authority?) by saying that every believer has that authority. The person who recognizes that we are all ministers and are called by God with our respective gifts and talents has that right. The person who spends time studying and rightly dividing the Word to show (him or herself) to be approved, who spends time talking to God and getting to know Him and the mysteries of His Kingdom (Eph.1) on a daily basis. That person who is maturing to a place where they can be looked to for wisdom and guidance; that person who has the relationship with God and the faith to be used of God, has the right to question. They also have the right to be used of God in whatever capacity He chooses them for.

Let's take a look at where this Nicolaitan thing started and how it has been used or misused over the ages. Let's also look at how Jesus took that responsibility of priesthood upon His own shoulders and transferred it to all of us to where we can now look to Him as our own personal High Priest (Heb. 4:14-15, 5:1-10, and 6:20) and Author and Finisher of our faith (Heb.12:2).

Chapter 2

PRIESTHOOD-101

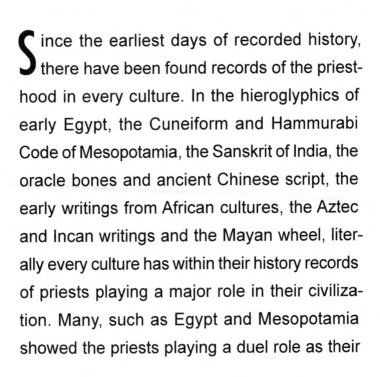

S ince the earliest days of recorded history, there have been found records of the priesthood in every culture. In the hieroglyphics of early Egypt, the Cuneiform and Hammurabi Code of Mesopotamia, the Sanskrit of India, the oracle bones and ancient Chinese script, the early writings from African cultures, the Aztec and Incan writings and the Mayan wheel, literally every culture has within their history records of priests playing a major role in their civilization. Many, such as Egypt and Mesopotamia showed the priests playing a duel role as their king. The belief was that they were direct descendants of the gods or were actually the gods themselves. This ties in with the teaching that comes from Genesis about the Nephilim.

The Nephilim

Genesis 6:4
The **Nephilim** were on the earth in those days—and also afterward—when the sons of God went to the daughters of humans and had children by them. They were the heroes of old, men of renown. (NIV)

The descendants of the "sons of God" who are believed to be the fallen angels who rebelled along with Lucifer, are believed by many to be these god/man priests. They are depicted in Egyptian hieroglyphics, and in drawings of other cultures that had no possible way of being connected with Egypt, as being elevated to a place of being worshipped. They are often drawn as being much larger than normal humans, often with large odd shaped heads. The Mayans, Incas, and Aztecs were only a few example cultures who used similar symbols. One common denominator that most accounts have is that they are shown giving homage to a large serpent; either a snake or a dragon. (I could write another book on this subject with extensive documentation, but I am only mentioning it at this time to bring out the origins of the Nicolaitan influence).

Another common denominator to this idea is the similarity of mythological accounts in other cultures. The Greeks have some of the most well-known myths involving the Titans, gods such as Zeus, Hades, Poseidon, etc. who had carnal encounters with desirable human women and had offspring such as Hercules. The Romans of course, adopted their deities and gave them different names. Then there were the Norse accounts with Odin being the father of Thor, Baldr, Loki, and so on. The Gilgamesh had similar epics of their hero-gods and, as most other cultures, had gods to represent most the different aspects of nature. Their stories include a flood that covered the whole earth. Again, this small sampling of historical examples included in every account, priests. The priests of these deities all required homage and sacrifice, not only to the deities, but to the priests themselves. Many times these sacrifices included humans, even children, as was known to be among Baal, Ashtoreth, and Molech worshipers in Canaan, as well as among the Aztecs in Mexico. **The bottom line is, these were priests of false gods, idols, fallen angels, and demons.** *The difference between these priests and priests of God is, these priests demanded servitude and God required his priests to be servants.*

God's Priests

Old Testament
Exodus 29:44

*So I will consecrate the tabernacle of meeting and the altar. I will also consecrate both Aaron and his sons to minister to Me as **priests**.*

The first duty of the priest of YHWH was to minister to Him. They were to be consecrated, or set apart, from everyone else to serve God, not themselves. In serving God, they served all the people as well. They made atonement for their sins by offering sacrifices and they were responsible for helping the people to be in a right relationship with God.

When the priests deviated from that duty, the result was disastrous. Jeremiah 5:31 says, *The prophets prophesy falsely, And the **priests** rule by their own power; And My people love to have it so. But what will you do in the end?*

Jeremiah was speaking judgment upon the false priests who would not only lose their priesthood, but would be judged in the end on judgment day. Examples of priests choosing to ignore God and serve themselves are found throughout Jeremiah and most of the Major Prophets. It is one of the main themes in the book of Ezekiel, however, a specific example can be found much earlier in I Samuel.

In I Samuel 2, beginning at verse 12, Eli's sons were wicked and had been taking more than their share of the sacrifices, consorting with temple prostitutes, worshiping false gods, etc. An unidentified "man of god" came along and prophesied against Eli and his sons. Against Eli, because of his refusing to do anything about it and against the sons because of their rebellion. The prophecy not only judged them, but the people of Israel. As a result, the sons were killed in battle, the Ark of the Covenant was taken away, the Israelites were defeated and

Eli fell backwards as a result of the shock of the news of his sons, and died of a broken neck. All of this happened because God's priests were not holy. They were not committed to living for Him, but for themselves.

The root of the problem lies in this verse-I Samuel 2:12-

Now the sons of Eli were corrupt; they did not know the Lord.

The first pre-requisite of a priest is that they must **know the Lord!** In the New Testament, the prerequisite of a Christian is that they must **know the Lord! The will of God is that every believer becomes a priest of God who knows the Lord!** The problem with the religion of the Nicolaitan is that it prevents people from knowing the Lord. It says that to know the Lord, you must go through them. This is why Jesus hates this belief, this doctrine, and this system. He wants to know each one of us as his own intimately! Eli's sons inherited the position of priests without having a relationship with the Lord. Thus, their position was merely a job, or career. Their actions were routine and were thought of as professional rather than devotional. They were false priests. The same tragedy has taken place throughout time and is still happening today. People are still being misled by these Nicolaitans who themselves, are motivated by selfishness rather than the love and wisdom of the Lord.

Chapter 3

THEIR TRUE COLORS

This story tells the difference between a true shepherd and a Nicolaitan:

A man was taking a guided tour of Israel and his tour guide was showing them the everyday lifestyle in one of the villages. The man on the tour asked the tour guide, "I have always heard that a shepherd leads his sheep rather than driving them. Why is this shepherd driving his sheep down that hill into a pen?" The tour guide answered, "That man is not a shepherd, he is a butcher."

The Nicolaitans are the butchers. They have no interest in the welfare of the sheep. They are not called, but call themselves to use the sheep to fulfill their own interests, such as power and control. Ezekiel describes them in chapter 34:

1And the word of the Lord came to me, saying, 2 "Son of man, prophesy against the shepherds of Israel, prophesy and say to them, 'Thus says the Lord God to the shepherds: "Woe to the shepherds of Israel who feed themselves! Should not the shepherds feed the flocks? 3 You eat the fat and clothe yourselves with the wool; you slaughter the fatlings, but you do not feed the flock. 4 The weak you have not strengthened, nor have you healed those who were sick, nor bound up the broken, nor brought back what was driven away, nor sought what was lost; but with force and cruelty you have ruled them. *5* *So they were scattered because there was no shepherd; and they became food for all the beasts of the field when they were scattered. 6 My sheep wandered through all the mountains, and on every high hill; yes, My flock was scattered over the whole face of the earth, and no one was seeking or searching for them."*

7 *'Therefore, you shepherds, hear the word of the Lord: 8 "As I live," says the Lord God, "surely because My flock became a prey, and My flock became food for every beast of the field, because there was no shepherd, nor did My shepherds search for My flock, but the shepherds fed themselves and did not feed My flock"— 9 therefore, O shepherds, hear the word of the Lord! 10 Thus says the Lord God: "Behold, I am against the shepherds, and I will require My flock at their hand; I will cause them to cease feeding the sheep, and the shepherds shall feed themselves no more; for I will deliver My flock from their mouths, that they may no longer be food for them.* God, the True Shepherd

11 *'For thus says the Lord God: "Indeed I Myself will search for My sheep and seek them out.* ***12*** *As a shepherd seeks out his flock on the day he is among his scattered sheep, so will I seek out My sheep and deliver them from all the places where they were scattered on a cloudy and dark day.* ***13*** *And I will bring them out from the peoples and gather them from the countries, and will bring them to their own land; I will feed them on the mountains of Israel, in the valleys and in all the inhabited places of the country.* ***14*** *I will feed them in good pasture, and their fold shall be on the high mountains of Israel. There they shall lie down in a good fold and feed in rich pasture on the mountains of Israel.* ***15*** *I will feed My flock, and I will make them lie down," says the Lord God.* ***16*** *"I will seek what was lost and bring back what was driven away, bind up the broken and strengthen* what was sick; but I will destroy the fat and the strong, and feed them in judgment."

17 'And as for you, O My flock, thus says the Lord God: "Behold, I shall judge between sheep and sheep, between rams and goats. **18** Is it too little for you to have eaten up the good pasture, that you must tread down with your feet the residue of your pasture—and to have drunk of the clear waters, that you must foul the residue with your feet? **19** And as for My flock, they eat what you have trampled with your feet, and they drink what you have fouled with your feet."

20 'Therefore thus says the Lord God to them: "Behold, I Myself will judge between the fat and the lean sheep. **21** Because you have pushed with side and shoulder, butted all the weak ones with your horns, and scattered them abroad, **22** therefore I will save My flock, and they shall no longer be a prey; and I will judge between sheep and sheep. **23** I will establish one shepherd over them, and he shall feed them—My servant David. He shall feed them and be their shepherd. **24** And I, the Lord, will be their God, and My servant David a prince among them; I, the Lord, have spoken.

25 "I will make a covenant of peace with them, and cause wild beasts to cease from the land; and they will dwell safely in the wilderness and sleep in the woods. **26** I will make them and the places all around My hill a blessing; and I will cause showers to come down in their season; there shall be showers of blessing. **27** Then the trees of the field shall yield their fruit, and the earth shall yield her increase. They shall be safe in their land; and they shall know that I am the Lord, when I have broken the bands of their yoke and delivered them from the hand of those who enslaved them. **28** And they shall no longer be a prey for the nations, nor shall beasts of the land devour them; but they shall dwell safely, and no one shall make them afraid. **29** I will raise up for them a garden of *renown, and they shall no longer be consumed with hunger in the land, nor bear the shame of the Gentiles anymore. 30 Thus they shall know that I, the Lord their God, am with them, and they, the house of Israel, are My people," says the Lord God.'*

31 "You are My flock, the flock of My pasture; you are men, and I am your God," says the Lord God."

Ezekiel shows the motivation and actions of the false shepherds, but it also shows God's intentions for his people. Ezekiel prophesied about the coming relationship between mankind and God under the New Covenant. Throughout the passage, the Lord reiterates that *He* will be their shepherd, their judge, their teacher, deliverer, their healer, and their God.

An interesting statement in verse 21 alludes to the corrupt shepherds "butting the weak ones with your horns..." which clearly shows that the shepherds are also sheep. That changes our concept of the shepherds being ministers and the parishioners being lowly sheep. It puts us all in the same category with some having one particular job or calling but each one as important as the other.

In these Scriptures, God is segueing into the New Covenant, showing his people what is to come. During the time of the Old Testament, God's priests still had to make atonement and sacrifices for the people to be able to be in right standing with God. However, each act of the offering of blood of the spotless lamb, bulls, goats, and doves; each act of cleansing and atonement, putting the sin on the head of the scapegoat, and all the other rituals had symbolic meaning that was foretelling the coming of the ultimate sacrifice, the Messiah.

The New Covenant is the culmination of the prophecies, the struggles, the victories, the defeats and the essence of the history of the Old Covenant. The New Covenant has one focal point. This focus is on a person; Jesus. At least 365 prophecies were made and fulfilled about Him. The blood on the doorposts during the Passover had the point intersects of a cross. Songs in the book of Psalms are chocked full of detailed prophecies of Jesus' life, crucifixion, resurrection, ascension, and return. No one can share the glory of our High Priest. No one even comes close to achieving that glory.

What Motivates Someone To Be A Nicolaitan?

The motivation behind such a desire is found in Isaiah 14 when Lucifer thought he should be like God. Isaiah prophesied in verses 12-15:

"How you are fallen from heaven,
O Lucifer,ʳ son of the morning!
How you are cut down to the ground,
You who weakened the nations!

44

¹³ For you have said in your heart:
'I will ascend into heaven,
I will exalt my throne above the stars of God;
I will also sit on the mount of the congregation
On the farthest sides of the north;
¹⁴ I will ascend above the heights of the clouds,
I will be like the Most High.'
¹⁵ Yet you shall be brought down to Sheol,
To the lowest depths of the Pit.

Lucifer's hubris caused him to fall and be known as Satan (the usurper). His first temptation of Adam and Eve included the phrase, "For God knows that in the day you eat of it your eyes will be opened, and you will be like God, knowing good and evil" (Genesis 3:5). The catch phrase or selling point of the original temptation that led to original sin was to "be like God". That temptation becomes the downfall of everyone who gets taken in by it. It is the underlying force behind the deeds and doctrines of the Nicolaitans. To establish someone to stand in the place of Jesus, of God incarnate, is the ultimate form of deadly pride. Jesus intends for all of us to have equal access to Him. **We should never be separated from Him after we have experienced his salvation. We should never have to access Him through someone else.**

I once told another minister that I hated to be called "reverend" because I thought there was only one person who deserved that title. The other minister responded, "Well, I think I earned that title when I graduated from (prestigious name) seminary." Herein lies the difference in thinking. The title "reverend" clearly indicates that a person should be revered. This reverence is earned through passing courses of higher learning and jumping through man-made hoops that are becoming more and more difficult to achieve. Unfortunately, the majority of these classes being taught in most mainstream

denominations are according to the "higher criticism" theology which tries to sow doubt and
downright unbelief in the students. So the outcome is, once you graduate with the indoctri-
nation of doubt and learn to use theology to
excuse unbelief, you earn the title "reverend".

The title "reverend" implies that one is set
apart and more "holy" or qualified to represent
the other "laypeople" before God. If this position had been based upon actions of self-sacri-
fice by preaching the Gospel to and taking care
of the needs of the poor and needy, it would
hold more credence. If it was based upon the
hours of prayer spent each day, regular fasting,
studying the Word of God and living a righteous
lifestyle, and above all, having a pure heart, the
title "reverend" might be more fitting. But even
then, that person would insist that the only one
who should be revered is Jesus Christ. These
things, however, are not what the modern
mainstream churches use to qualify one to be

called "reverend". The seminary degrees that have been obtained through the constant bombardment of doubt and unbelief, and more often than not, result in a spiritual pride that elevates one's self above those who have not obtained these degrees, are what "qualifies" the entitlement of "reverend". I have often been questioned and scrutinized in such a way that would try to find error in my approach to ministry by some who openly admit that they do not believe the Bible is the written Word of God. Some of these who scrutinized me were also, unashamedly, walking in lifestyles that did not align with Scripture.

It is scriptural and good to be held accountable in one's ministry to make sure that ministry is walking in accordance to God's word. Some of the questions asked should be:

- Are you studying the Bible daily?
- Do you have a daily time of prayer and communion with God?

- Do you visit the sick, shut-ins, those who need evangelism and counsel?

- Are you ministering to the poor and needy?

- Are you leading the people into more powerful and genuine worship?

- What has God been showing you recently?

- What revelations, miracles, or answers to prayer have you experienced lately?

- Are more people in your church discovering and moving in their gifts?

...and the list goes on. Rather, we are constantly reminded to align with denominational doctrinal boundaries that conflict with Scripture and were rooted in Nicolaitan doctrine such as infant baptism (not believer's baptism which is the only one supported by Scriptural examples). We are scrutinized pertaining to matters of money while never asked about how many souls were saved. Those who jump through all the proper hoops without questioning things that are obviously wrong are usually the ones rewarded with the most prestigious and high paying positions. After the unfathomable amount of time and work of completing assignments and tasks so as to finally be rewarded with the title, "ordained", that person feels as if they have earned the title. After that, the temptation is to fear speaking out or acting upon one's true convictions in fear of losing all that they have worked for. The bottom line is, Satan wants to make sure those in charge are motivated by a desire to have more power and control just as he is. He knows that he can take down a good organization or system if it just has the wrong leadership led by the wrong motives.

Matthew 23:1-12 Then Jesus spoke to the multitudes and to His disciples, ² saying: "The scribes and the Pharisees sit in Moses' seat. ³ Therefore whatever they tell you to observe, that observe and do, but do not do according *to their works; for they say, and do not do. ⁴ For they bind heavy burdens, hard to bear, and lay them on men's shoulders; but they themselves will not move them with one of their fingers. ⁵ But all their works they do to be seen by men. They make their phylacteries broad and enlarge the borders of their garments. ⁶ They love the best places at feasts, the best seats in the syn- agogues, ⁷ greetings in the marketplaces, and to be called by men, 'Rabbi, Rabbi.' ⁸ **But you, do not be called 'Rabbi'; for One is your Teacher, the Christ, and you are all brethren. ⁹ Do not call anyone on earth your father; for One is your Father, He who is in heaven. 10 And do not be called teachers; for One is your Teacher, the Christ.** ¹¹ But he who is greatest among you shall be your servant. ¹² And who- ever exalts himself will be humbled, and he who humbles himself will be exalted.*

The names, "reverend", "father", "priest", etc. all imply that this person is a mediator that one must go through to have an audience with God. The beauty of true Christianity is that each and every one of us has access to the throne of grace. Everyone that belongs to Christ and has a personal relationship with Him has the enduement of power from on high to fulfill individual ministries that God has given us. To place one on a higher plane than others and give them a title to imply that they are closer to God, why not just give them the title, "Nicolaitan"?

Now that we have an idea of who the Nicolaitans are and why Jesus hated their deeds, let us discover who they were during the time of Jesus' ministry on the earth. I believe the answer is simple and obvious as they were regularly trying to oppose the works of Christ and the will of God because it interfered with their agenda and contradicted their purpose.

Chapter 4

THE NICOLAITANS DURING JESUS TIME

The Nicolaitans had a stronghold on the Jews during the time of Jesus life on earth. As the Jews were being oppressed by the Romans with no freedom and under constant scrutiny and fear, it was not a new phenomenon to them. The priests and temple rulers already had that kind of control without the help of the Romans. The Romans were the clear representation of the world system. Jesus regularly spoke of "the world" and how we are to be separate and not conformed to this world. In Matthew

13:22, He refers to the cares of this world. In Matthew 18:7, Jesus says "woe to the world because of offenses...", in John 8:23, Jesus said that He was not of this world, and in John 12:31, He says, "Now is the judgment of this world; now the ruler of this world will be cast out." We also remember that Jesus came into the world to save it because of God's love for it (John 3:16-17).

The irony is though, that the religious system was also opposed to Jesus ministry and the will of God in general. What was more ominous and deadly was that the people were to believe that the religious leaders represented God and they were supposed to be the "good guys". The Pharisees, Sadducees, Priests, and temple officials had a grip of fear on the people. They had become entangled with the politics of religion based upon desire for power and control, all having the appearance of godliness, but without the love and kindness that should accompany it. If the leaders had been like the godly men of the past, when the enemies of Rome came, they should have inspired the people to pray and seek God's face and repent as Joshua, Samuel, David, Hezekiah, Gideon, and many others did. Instead, they sided with the world system as the unfaithful and compromising kings, prophets and priests of old did. **The outcome of the religious system and the world was the same in dealing with Jesus. Both the Jewish leaders and Rome were equally responsible for the crucifixion.**

The evidence that reveals the identity of the Nicolaitans during the time of Jesus life on earth is shown clearly in their conflicts with Him. I sometimes automatically defer to the name, "Pharisee" and use it interchangeably with Nicolaitan when discussing the New Testament, but that is not completely accurate. There were the Sadducees who did not believe in the resurrection (that is why they were sad, you see), the priests, which included the high priest and other temple rulers.

It is important to note that there was somewhat of a variety of the Nicolaitans during Jesus time just as there is now. It is also important to know that although all the Pharisees and Sadducees were in the Nicolaitan mindset, all of them were not Nicolaitans. The Scripture implied that Nicodemus ventured out of their way of thinking in John 3 when he was asking Jesus how one could enter the Kingdom of Heaven. The Scripture says that he met Jesus in secret and wanted to know how to have eternal life. Had the other Pharisees known that, Nicodemus would have probably been excommunicated from the Temple. Nicodemus recognized that Jesus had the answer, or even more, was the source of eternal life and was truly the Messiah.

Another Pharisee who knew that Jesus was the Messiah was a man named Saul. In Acts chapter 9, Saul was as zealous as one could be toward the Nicolaitan way of thinking, advocating the control and power of the Pharisees and holding many Christians hostage in fear of persecution for following whom he thought was a dissident and heretic named Jesus who was responsible for this "cult" called "The Way". On the road to Damascus, he was knocked down and blinded by the Glory of God and Jesus himself spoke to him. Saul suddenly converted from a Nicolaitan to a follower of Christ with the new name of Paul. His new name showed that he had a new identity with Christ, or a new life and way of thinking. In one moment, he found that the way to eternal life and God himself was to know Him personally.

The Bible implies that there were other religious as well as political leaders who were inclined to believe in Jesus. Joseph of Arimathea was the most well-known example of a political leader who was a follower of Christ. In Matthew

27 and John 19, he offered his own tomb up for Jesus burial. There was the Roman centurion whose servant was healed in Matthew 8. Jesus spoke of this gentile as having more faith than the Jews. **All who were in secular or religious authority were not Nicolaitans. It was only the ones whose hearts were bent towards power and control.**

Jesus, Head-to-Head With the Nicolaitans

We will look at several examples of the direct conflict between Jesus and the Nicolaitans. Each example will show how the root of the conflict was caused by the Nicolaitans feeling threatened that they will lose their power and control.

The temple rulers and sects such as the Pharisees and Sadducees were the ones who always opposed Jesus and the work of God. They were also the ones in power with the knowledge that they had control over the people because of their fear of eternal damnation, life and death, and being cursed or blessed. These were the priests, the mediators between the layperson and God. If the religious leaders were opposed or offended, they had the power to throw you out of the synagogue and separate you from God. Jesus came and offered them life, hope, and healing. This was a real threat to the Pharisees and temple rulers. Jesus always had opposition from this group who were a perfect fit to the definition of the Nicolaitans. Jesus came to set the people free from that kind of bondage and give them access to God.

Let's look at several Scriptural examples of the Nicolaitan conflict with Jesus in the Gospels. In Matthew 23, Jesus described them in this manner: *Then Jesus spoke to the multitudes and to His disciples, saying: "The scribes and the Pharisees sit in Moses' seat. Therefore whatever they tell you to observe, that observe and do, but do not do according to their works, for they say, and do not do. ...".* Jesus did not take away from the authority given them by God under the old covenant. He did, however reveal that their hearts and motives were not right. They would have fit under the adage of "don't do what I do, do what I say.

In Matthew 5:20, Jesus said, "For I say to you, that unless your righteousness exceeds the righteousness of the scribes and Pharisees, you will by no means enter the kingdom of heaven." The Nicolaitans would have the people believe that they were righteous and perfect in every way however Jesus knew their hearts and their actions in secret. They were the example of religion and He was the epitome of what a relationship with God really was. Today, we still have that conflict between "religion" and "relationship" in the Church. Later, we will discuss how that conflict was caused by the infiltration of the Nicolaitans' doctrine and actions in the Church.

Although this parable is usually used to teach humility, Luke 18 shows the difference between surface religion, based upon bad motives verses a true desire to seek God's love. The story goes like this:

The Parable of the Pharisee and the Tax Collector

Luke 18:9 *Also He spoke this parable to some who trusted in themselves that they were righteous, and despised others:* **10** *"Two men went up to the temple to pray, one a Pharisee and the other a tax collector.* **11** *The Pharisee stood and prayed thus with himself, 'God, I thank You that I am not like other men—extortioners, unjust, adulterers, or even as this tax collector.* **12** *I fast twice a week; I give tithes of all that I possess.'* **13** *And the tax collector, standing afar off, would not so much as raise his eyes to heaven, but beat his breast, saying,*

'God, be merciful to me a sinner!' **14** *I tell you,
this man went down to his house justified rather
than the other; for everyone who exalts himself
will be humbled, and he who humbles himself
will be exalted.*

The tax collector (which included Matthew
and Zacchaeus) needed nothing short of direct
access to God. According to Jesus, he had
exactly that. His audience with God was granted
by humility and a sincere heart, not by going
through someone else, who had the proper
"credentials". This is the heart of the message
that Jesus brought to the world during his walk
on earth. He showed us that God's love came
down to us so we could have that fellowship
with Him that we were originally intended to
have. God wants us to walk with Him and talk
with Him in the same intimate fellowship that
was between He and Adam in the garden.

Jesus made it clear that even though the
Pharisee had an impressive prayer, it did

not reach Heaven. The Pharisee may have impressed men, but he did not move God. The tax collector's prayer moved upon God's heart and got results; God's mercy and forgiveness. James 5:16 says that the *...effective, fervent prayer of a righteous man avails much.* How powerful prayers would be if everyone could realize that they have direct access to the throne room of God! I am convinced that if a body of believers would trust God to hear them rather than allowing the "professional pray-er" to do it all, that we would regularly see miracles, answers to prayer and revival. It would not even seem unusual to us. Clearly the doctrine of the Nicolaitans has weakened the effectiveness of this.

NIT PICKING AND JEALOUSY

The Gospels are full of examples where the religious leaders revealed their true motives when they encountered Jesus. They saw that He was the real thing and that they did not have what He had. They saw that they were losing control of the people as they chose to follow Him. Their plan was falling apart and all their paradigms were shifting because of this one Rabbi. Something had to be done. Perhaps they could find some fault, some loop-hole, in what He was doing that would expose Him as a charlatan. If that didn't work, they could create a fault that they could use to justify removing Him once and for all. These motives did not contain one molecule of anything righteous, holy, or good. Yet, their intention was to prove themselves as "right" and the author of all that is good, wrong.

Excommunication of the Blind Man

In John 9, Jesus had healed a blind man by making some clay with some dust and his own spittle and putting it on the man's eyes. This man had been blind from birth and was given his eyesight. This particular miracle had never before been performed by anyone throughout Scripture. The significance of Jesus forming clay from his own body fluid is reminiscent of the creation of Adam in Genesis when God created him out of the dust of the ground. This clearly signifies that Jesus did a creative miracle, giving the man eyes that he never had. The one catch, that I believe was intentional, was that Jesus performed this miracle on the Sabbath. In verse 16, the Pharisees said, "This Man is not from God, because He does not keep the Sabbath." **The Pharisees were more concerned that Jesus had performed a miracle on the Sabbath than that He had done a creative miracle and gave a man sight.** This shows that the motivation of the Nicolaitan thinker is always directed at "self" or "me" and has no regard for any other human being. They knew that the people would want to follow this Messiah and that they would no longer have any control over the people. Their reaction was to excommunicate the formerly blind man and seek to destroy Jesus. This next exchange of Scripture details the Pharisees' reaction:

John 9:24 *So they again called the man who was blind, and said to him, "Give God the glory! We know that this Man is a sinner."*

25 He answered and said, "Whether He is a sinner or not I do not know. One thing I know: that though I was blind, now I see."

26 Then they said to him again, "What did He do to you? How did He open your eyes?"

27 He answered them, "I told you already, and you did not listen. Why do you want to hear it again? Do you also want to become His disciples?"

28 Then they reviled him and said, "You are His disciple, but we are Moses' disciples. 29

We know that God spoke to Moses; as for this fellow, we do not know where He is from."

30 The man answered and said to them, "Why, this is a marvelous thing, that you do not know where He is from; yet He has opened my eyes! 31 Now we know that God does not hear sinners; but if anyone is a worshiper of God and does His will, He hears him. 32 Since the world began it has been unheard of that anyone opened the eyes of one who was born blind. 33 If this Man were not from God, He could do nothing."

34 They answered and said to him, "You were completely born in sins, and are you teaching us?" And they cast him out.

Where is any evidence of the true nature of God or his love in the Pharisees? The only thing they were concerned about was that everyone still recognized their establishment of priesthood and power over the people. Forget the fact that Jesus just did a miracle that has never been recorded before! They were going to keep that man in his proper place. They missed the Kingdom of God by as far as the East is from the West. The good news is, when the man was ostracized out of their kingdom, God took him into His!

Chapter 5

THE RISE OF THE NICOLAITANS IN THE CHURCH

The warning from Jesus, mentioned earlier, from Revelation 2 shows that the Nicolaitan spirit had already been creeping into the church. I cannot emphasize enough how important it was for Jesus to address it from the throne room of God as a problem in two of the seven churches of Asia. Of the warnings of idolatry, immorality, Satanism, lukewarmness, losing their first love, etc., the doctrines and deeds of the Nicolaitans ranked right up there with them. We need to look at the events in history that not only back this statement up, but show the ongoing struggle taking place within the Church even today. But first, let us start with the early Church.

Two Histories

If you want an accurate depiction of the early Church, simply look at the book of Acts. We have a double benefit in reading this book because it was written by "Dr. Luke", who was a stickler for detail, plus Luke was driven and guided by the Holy Spirit. The disciples were everyday people who had been transformed into new creations. These "everyday people" were now being led and empowered by the Holy Spirit every day and God's guidance and miracles were being seen every day. This intensified their everyday experiences to where the miracles, blessings, trials, persecutions, challenges, etc. were far beyond "everyday".

The first such incident happened on the day of Pentecost, when the believers continually and faithfully sought God, and the "promise of the Father" that Jesus admonished them to seek in the last chapter of Luke and the first chapter of Acts. Not only did the wind blow and the fire fell and the people began to speak in tongues, but they were transformed and enabled to do what Jesus had called them to do. Peter, who once denied Jesus, stood in the midst of the very crowd that chanted, "Crucify Him", and preached the gospel boldly, accusing the people of killing the Messiah. About three thousand believers were added to the Church that day, and that was only the beginning.

The Nicolaitan "History"

The Nicolaitan history reminds me of the "Bizarro World" found in the *Superman® comics,* where there is an alternative Superman with

71

alternative values, motives, and language. The history that the Nicolaitans concoct is just as bizarre. I recently read a newspaper article about a pastor of a congregation, who described her type of worship as "Pauline". This worship that she described was serene, liturgical, ritualistic, and rather boring. Her philosophy approved of sins that Paul adamantly preached against, and it substituted ritual for repentance liturgy for new life. Her description of "worship", which she blamed on Paul, frankly painted a picture of Paul as a "sissy", who wore long robes and chanted ancient Latin choruses.

The Real Paul

Let's take a look at the apostle Paul, as he describes his life in 2 Corinthians 11:*22-33:*

Are they Hebrews? So am I. Are they Israelites? So am I. Are they the seed of Abraham? So am I. 23 Are they ministers of Christ?—I speak as a fool—I am more: in labors more abundant, in stripes above measure, in prisons more frequently, in deaths often. 24 From the Jews five times I received forty stripes minus one. 25 Three times I was beaten with rods; once I was stoned; three times I was shipwrecked; a night and a day I have been in the deep; 26 in journeys often, in perils of waters, in perils of robbers, in perils of my own countrymen, in perils of the Gentiles, in perils in the city, in perils in the wilderness, in perils in the sea, in perils among false brethren; 27 in weariness and toil, in sleeplessness often, in hunger and thirst, in fastings often, in cold and nakedness— 28 besides the other things, what comes upon me daily: my deep concern for all the churches. 29 Who is weak, and I am not weak? Who is made to stumble, and I do not burn with indignation?

***30** If I must boast, I will boast in the things which concern my infirmity. **31** The God and Father of our Lord Jesus Christ, who is blessed forever, knows that I am not lying. **32** In Damascus the governor, under Aretas the king, was guarding the city of the Damascenes with a garrison, desiring to arrest me; **33** but I was let down in a basket through a window in the wall, and escaped from his hands.*

Paul had many more trials and tribulations, including the one described in Acts 27 and 28 about being stranded at sea in a storm for weeks on a ship: floating in the sea, holding onto debris, after the ship wrecked; rescued by the natives on an island, only to be bitten by a viper while throwing a stick on the fire. The natives assumed he must be a criminal or murderer until he had no reaction to the poisonous snake; then they though he was a god.

Those of us who grew up in the rural country would refer to Paul as one who was "rode hard and put up wet." He was definitely not the "pristine Paul" who was described by this pastor. Unfortunately, her view of Paul was shaped by one of the many seminaries that have been influenced by the Nicolaitan teaching. Spiritually, Paul was also not the quiet and serene individual that he was accused of being. He would preach in public squares and synagogues until he was driven out of town or beaten and imprisoned. He definitely did not have a boring, ritualistic manner of worship. He describes one of his worship encounters as follows:

2 Corinthians 12:1 *It is doubtless not profitable for me to boast. I will come to visions and revelations of the Lord: 2 I know a man in Christ who fourteen years ago—whether in the body I*

do not know, or whether out of the body I do not know, God knows—such a one was caught up to the third heaven. 3 And I know such a man—whether in the body or out of the body I do not know, God knows— 4 how he was caught up into Paradise and heard inexpressible words, which it is not lawful for a man to utter. 5 Of such a one I will boast; yet of myself I will not boast, except in my infirmities. 6 For though I might desire to boast, I will not be a fool; for I will speak the truth. But I refrain, lest anyone should think of me above what he sees me to be or hears from me.

I am envious of Paul's prayer time if this is an indicator of his daily devotions. This encounter rivals that of Jesus on the mount of transfiguration when He was communing with Moses and Elijah. To be honest, Paul would not fit in a formal, ritualistic, liturgical worship service. He would more than likely add that to the list of his tribulations and admonish them to "**Rejoice in**

the Lord always. Again I will say, rejoice!" (Philippians 4:4)

Other disciples of Christ are also given a false image in this Nicolaitan bizarro-world. The most misconstrued and misrepresented is probably Peter. I see no evidence that when Peter was transformed by the Holy Spirit on the day of Pentecost, he suddenly took on a papal hat, scepter, and gown. He still probably was dressed as a fisherman and looked like an everyday person. In **Acts 4:13** the Scripture says,

"Now when they saw the boldness of Peter and John, and perceived that they were **uneducated** and **untrained** men, they marveled. And they realized that they had been with Jesus."

This is the only defining difference that made Peter, James, John, and others stand out from the ordinary people of the day. They had "been with Jesus". The people could see Jesus in their lives, actions, and countenance. None of them appeared to be "religious" or ecclesiastical. They were fishermen, tax collectors, construction workers, laborers, tent makers, who had love and compassion for their brothers and sisters in the Lord and the lost people around them. None of them floated around in long robes and funny hats chanting in Latin. Many of them did speak in other tongues of men and angels. Many prophesied, cast out demons, healed the sick, preached, taught, worked miracles, raised the dead, etc., because the Spirit of the Living God indwelled in them. This would not have happened if they were unable to have a personal encounter with God, with Jesus, with the Holy Spirit. This experience did not happen because they went through a priest, bishop, "ordained elder", or "deacon". It happened because they met the High Priest himself; Jesus Christ. The Nicolaitan doctrine is intended to prevent people from having a personal relationship with Jesus Christ. That is why Jesus said He hated it.

The previous misconception of Peter emerged from a false teaching that came from an errant interpretation of Matthew 16:18 when Jesus said,

Blessed are you, Simon Bar-Jonah, for flesh and blood has not revealed this to you, but My Father who is in heaven. And I also say to you that you are Peter, and on this rock I will build My church, and the gates of Hades shall not prevail against it. And I will give you the keys to the kingdom of heaven, and whatever you bind on earth will be bound in heaven, and whatever you loose on earth will be loosed in heaven. Then He commanded His disciples that they should tell no one that He was Jesus the Christ.

The misconception here is that Jesus was calling Peter the rock that the church would be built upon. The word in the Greek for Peter was *petros,* which is a masculine version of the name rock. When Jesus said, "on this rock", the word for "rock" was *petra,* which is the feminine form of the word. The Church was always referred to in the feminine sense (i.e. "the Bride of Christ). Jesus was referring to Peter as a "rock" or a building stone in the church. The "rock" that Jesus was referring to building the church upon was the confession that Peter made which was "You are the Christ, the Son of the living God."

Psalm 118:22, Matthew 21:42, Mark 12:10, Luke 20:17, Acts 4:11, 1 Peter 2:6,7 all refer to Jesus as the "chief cornerstone" that was rejected by the builders, but you must believe on Him to be saved. **Notice that Peter himself refers to Jesus as the "chief cornerstone" twice, reaffirming that it is Jesus, not Peter who is the "rock" on which the Church is built.** The way we become one of the building stones in the Church is to *believe* in that Cornerstone, Jesus Christ. **The Nicolaitans have turned**

the very one who first confessed Jesus as the Messiah into an idol to be worshipped, a priest to pray to so as to have access to Jesus or the Father. That is so much like the tactics that the devil loves to use; that is, to try to reverse and even mock what God has done to steal His glory and corrupt His creation. Peter, himself would remind us to read what Paul said to Timothy in 1 Timothy 2:5: *For there is one God and one Mediator between God and men, the Man Christ Jesus.*

In 2 Timothy 3:5, Paul defined the Nicolaitan or person with religion and no relationship. After a long list of sins for a believer to turn from, the last one mentioned was, "having a form of godliness, but denying its power. And from such people, turn away." One such character was described in the book of III John when John said,

9 I wrote to the church, but Diotrephes, who loves to have the preeminence among them, does not receive us. 10 Therefore, if I come, I will call to mind his deeds which he does, prating against us with malicious words. And not content with that, he himself does not receive the brethren, and forbids those who wish to, putting them out of the church.

This Diotrephes got caught up in the power of the position and felt threatened by John's letter and the possibility of him coming. This Diotrephes, resisted the admonition to the Church from the apostle John, who leaned upon the breast of Jesus at the last supper. The difference between a called leader and a Nicolaitan is clearly portrayed here. John, encouraging his fellow servants in love, verses Diotrephes who is threatening them and throwing them out of the church if they do not obey him. This depicts a vivid scene of the shepherd leading the flock and a butcher driving them. What is the fine line between the two? **Motive**! One is to love and obey God and serve others; the other is to serve one's self. That has always been the motive that separates the sheep from the goats. That is what separates the Nicolaitan from the called servant of God.

When The Nicolaitans Doctrine Took Hold

Throughout the 2nd century, A.D., Christianity grew and spread through the preaching of the Gospel and the fellowship of the saints. Churches would be established as a result of apostles, prophets, and evangelists spreading the Word. Persecution would occur, driving the local church either underground or to the next locale. Whether the spread of the Gospel was in a positive or negative manner, the Church was spreading and growing. Pastors and teachers would continue to feed the flocks and keep the believers on task. Local churches and peer relationships helped keep each other in check. When the size of the church grew, more rules were put into place which seemed to make it easier to control the masses than relying upon love and peer-accountability. (Does this sound familiar?) If you study the history of your own denomination, you will find that this trend occurs everywhere. It is human nature. You will see the same pattern in the Old Testament when the Israelites would follow Yahweh, get comfortable and start to focus upon themselves rather than God or each other, then they would fall away. The same pattern hit the Church as a whole and it repeats even after great revivals and awakenings. Most denominations were birthed after an awakening or reformation of some sort. Then they will begin to wane until there is another revival within that denomination. Then there will be another awakening or a division where some will stay and others will form another group. **When the "waning" or "lukewarmness" occurs within a church or denomination, you will find that at the**

beginnings of it, there was a Nicolaitan. This is not to say that this was all caused by the Nicolaitan, but that the heresies, strife, or luke-warmness that was there, opened the door for a strong leader or group of leaders to come in and "straighten things out".

When Jesus addressed the Church (via the seven churches of Asia) in Revelation 2 and 3, He saw a panoramic, yet detailed view of what was right and wrong with the Church. He was able to see it as a whole and He was able to see the secret thoughts of each individual. Jesus could see the seeds of everything that Satan would try to plant like weeds to choke out the good fruit of God's Church. Jesus was telling the Church to pull out those weeds that were sown in the midst of all the good works that were going on.

Although there were other church leaders, elders, bishops, (all synonyms from the same root word, *episkopos,* meaning overseer, or guardian), besides Diotrephes, who were "lording it over" their churches, this was kept in check for the most part until around the third century. Certain heresies were becoming widespread that were dividing the Church and needed to be squelched. There was a controversy over the Trinity between Arius and some of his followers vs. Alexander and the majority of the bishops of his era. Arius, Eusebius, and some other popular leaders were spreading the doctrine that Jesus was created by the Father because the Scripture used the term, "begotten", therefore He had a beginning and an end. The rest of the church held to the early church belief that the Father, Son, and Holy Spirit were one, yet separate and that Jesus was the *Logos* (Word) within the Father from the beginning (One source where you may find this is www.christian-history.org).

Jesus confirmed that in John 8:58 when He said, "Most assuredly, I say to you, before

Abraham was, I AM." What it really came down to was that one group was trying to understand the Bible with man's understanding and another was realizing that God cannot be understood, but rather *believed.* Paul said in 1 Corinthians 2:14 and 15, *But the natural man does not receive the things of the Spirit of God, for they are foolishness to him; nor can he know them, because they are spiritually discerned. But he who is spiritual judges all things, yet he himself is rightly judged by no one.*

The result of this controversy was that the emperor, Constantine called for a counsel to resolve the argument. This Counsel of Nicea was intended to heal the rift that was dividing the Church. The only agreement made was between the majority of bishops who decided to adopt the Nicene Creed which proclaimed that there was a Trinity and that the Father, Son, and Holy Spirit were one, yet separate and that the Son had existed within the Father since eternity past. Arius and Eusebius were quickly dividing the Church as the empire was also divided under Constantine. Constantine moderated the Counsel of Nicene and brought about a mutual agreement where the Nicene Creed was written. This seemed like a happy ending, but there was constant turmoil over this issue throughout the rule of Constantine. Constantine's son, Constantius, leaned toward the teachings of Arius and used his imperial power to remove and appoint bishops. At this juncture of history (around 325 A.D.), the politics of the world and the leadership of the Church began to overlap. This is when we see the beginning the corruption of the clergy, the pollution of power, and the separation of the saints. At this time, the overseers of the Church became elevated to a position of power and the separation of the "clergy" and "laity" began to become the rule of thumb. After this, the bishops or overseers became mediators and priests. Priests began to be called "father" even though Jesus clearly said in Matthew 23:9, "Do not call anyone on earth your father; for One is your Father, He who is in heaven."

When Constantine was on his deathbed in 337, he was finally baptized as a Christian. He was very much in favor of Christians during his reign because their beliefs were extremely beneficial to his empire. Their numbers were even more beneficial. He would have water sprinkled on troops as they would march to battle and on masses to do group "baptisms". When he and his son learned how to put pressure on the clergy who had ultimate control over the masses, they were able to rule the people without having to enforce them militarily. When the clergy were granted this political power, their eyes drifted from the service of God and the people to the enhancement of their own power, increase, and comfort. **Thus began the ultimate takeover of the Nicolaitans.**

Later in history, whenever there would be an awakening or revival, many times the leaders of the reform would be banished, executed or excommunicated. Most often, all or part of the confrontation would be centered around challenging the authority of the religious leaders. Much of the time, these religious leaders would be appointed by a political leader or another religious leader who was corrupt. When I say corrupt, I mean the person or persons would use the office or ministry for their own gain or advancement. The focus would always be on self rather than on the will of God or on others.

As I mentioned before, in the early church and today as well, the one factor that affects whether a movement or tradition is from man or from God, is called, *motive.* Is a decision being made after much prayer, confirmation from Scripture, agreement with others who are also committed to prayer, and reaffirming those people, or is it made at the advice of people with impure or selfish motives? I have seen churches, ministries, and movements fail because the motives were wrong. The bottom line is; do you want the ministry to be blessed my men or by God? Decisions that are made by worldly wisdom are like unto Abraham and Hagar, whereas actions taken by obedience to God and by faith are like Abraham and Sarah. That occurred because of direct communication between Abraham and God, not the advice of a committee (as are all decisions that are blessed by God.)

Chapter 6

NICOLAITANS TODAY

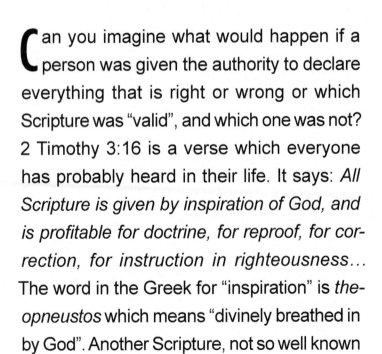

Can you imagine what would happen if a person was given the authority to declare everything that is right or wrong or which Scripture was "valid", and which one was not? 2 Timothy 3:16 is a verse which everyone has probably heard in their life. It says: *All Scripture is given by inspiration of God, and is profitable for doctrine, for reproof, for correction, for instruction in righteousness…* The word in the Greek for "inspiration" is *theopneustos* which means "divinely breathed in by God". Another Scripture, not so well known in Job 32:8 says, *But there is a spirit in man, And the breath of the Almighty gives him understanding.* Interestingly, the King James Version used the word "inspiration" where the word, "breath" is used in that verse. The Hebrew word *neshama* means "strong wind or breath of the Lord." The Greek phrase is also a derivative of the word *pneuma* which means "Spirit" and is also interchanged with "wind" or "breath". 1 Corinthians 2:12-16 says, *Now we have received, not the spirit of the world, but the Spirit who is from God, that we might know the things that have been freely given to us by God.*

13 These things we also speak, not in words which man's wisdom teaches but which the Holy Spirit teaches, comparing spiritual things with spiritual. 14 But the natural man does not receive the things of the Spirit of God, for they are foolishness to him; nor can he know them, because they are spiritually discerned. 15 But he who is spiritual judges all things, yet he him-self is rightly judged by no one. **16** *For 'who has known the mind of the Lord that he may instruct Him?' But we have the mind of Christ."*

These verses are saying:

- *All* Scripture is inspired by God and inter-woven and made alive by his Spirit.
- This is available to *all* of us, not a chosen few.
- It can only be received and understood by those whom God's Spirit resides in, not by natural or worldly intelligence.
- The only way to understand it is to have the Spirit of God, therefore one must *believe* to understand it. It is foolishness to everyone else.

There is a movement that has been around for a long time to discredit the Word of God or to take it out of the hands of the believer and convince us that we are not "qualified" to understand it. This same Nicolaitan spirit that existed during the time of the Pharisees (and before) exists now. It actually began in Genesis 3 when the serpent made Adam and Eve doubt God's Word and credibility. "Old What's His Name" has been trying to call God a liar since the beginning. The irony of that is that the devil is called the "father of liars". Jesus said in John 8:44- *You are of your father the devil, and the desires of your father you want to do. He was a murderer from the beginning, and does not stand in the truth, because there is no truth in him. When he speaks a lie, he speaks from his own resources, for he is a liar and the father of it*. Jesus was addressing the Pharisees during this conversation. It still applies today.

One of the main purposes of the Nicolaitans is to discredit God's word; either by lying about it, or by keeping it away from His people.

The way the Nicolaitan keeps the true believer from God's word is to convince us that we are not "qualified" to understand it, teach it, or convey it in any other way. The irony of this is that the majority of mainstream seminaries today teach God's Word as if it is not. They try to analytically tear the Scripture down with unbelief. Many times, I have heard professors say that things "contradicted" or were not accurate when it would be their limited understanding that did not comprehend it. The reason for that was that they were trying to critique God's word without the inspiration of the Spirit which 1Corinthians 2 talked about. The result of this is, students would agree with this false teaching, make a good grade, and be deemed "qualified" because they passed their seminary course with flying colors. They would go and preach this to a congregation and wonder why the congregation was "dying". They were dying because there was no life; there was no life because there was no Spirit (breath) of God; there was no Spirit because there was no faith. There was no faith because, *So then faith comes by hearing, and hearing by the word of God.* (Romans 10:17).

I had different professors say that their purpose was to systematically "tear down our belief system" so we could decide what we wanted to believe and establish our own faith. That sounds pretty good to an 18-year-old who first left home on their own and wants to prove to the world they can make it without anyone's help. They went on to say that we needed to forget everything our parents or grandparents taught us and discover what we would believe on our own (whatever happened to *Faith of Our Fathers*?) I remember a beautiful, sweet young girl (we'll call her Mary) who came from a small town in Tennessee who came to a particular school because her parents entrusted her to a "Christian college". This college preferred to be

97

called a liberal arts college rather than "Christian" even though it taught ministry courses. Mary was a wholesome, modest girl who was an "A" student with a lot of hope and plans for her future. I remember hearing her talking to her friends one day on the front porch of her dormitory near the end of the first semester. She said, "When I came here, I believed in the Bible, in miracles, and the things I was taught in Sunday School. Now I realize that they were not true and I don't believe in that anymore." By the end of her first year in college, she was living in one of the boy's fraternity houses, failing classes, and using drugs and alcohol. She trusted these professors as some sort of mediator in her life who must know what the truth is. They enjoyed having that power to influence young people's lives. What they don't realize is, even though this feeling of power is a great boost to their ego, it will not bode so well with their eternity.

Jesus warned:

Matthew 18:6 *Whoever causes one of these little ones who believe in Me to sin, it would be better for him if a millstone were hung around his neck, and he were drowned in the depth of the sea.*

The example I just shared, is not only the story of one girl, but also the story of thousands of people who have passed through classes like the ones I described in colleges and seminaries (or rather "cemeteries") all around the world and have been taught the same thing.

I was fortunate enough to have a great uncle, Dr. H. Thornton Fowler, who spent time with me and advised me on many occasions when I first felt called to preach. Uncle Thornton was a pastor of large congregations, a district superintendent, director of the United Methodist Publishing House, and many other roles in the United Methodist Church. He was sought after often as an evangelist at revivals and was once a candidate for bishop. I was privileged to know several people who were leaders in my church while growing up who were born-again at some of his revival meetings. Uncle Thornton warned me when I first started the ministry, to beware of the teachings in the colleges and seminaries. He is the one who I first heard use the term, "cemetery" rather than seminary in his sermons. He went into detail about how they would try to turn me from believing in the Bible as the word of God and he played a large part in helping me to stand firm.

During the early days of my schooling, many of my peers had the same warnings from their mentors, unfortunately, we are in a generation where those warnings are not as prevalent or they are simply just not heeded. I have person-ally warned young people going into training for the ministry, being reassured that they would not waver. Sadly, some of them have come out, not only not believing in the validity of God's Word, but doubting the very existence of God. Some left the ministry and others kept preaching while doubting. The latter is more tragic than the former because they, too, are leading others astray.

James 3:1 says, *My brethren, let not many of you become **teachers**, knowing that we shall receive a stricter judgment.* If the Bible is not true to you, if you do not believe in its inspiration, or if you cannot believe that it is God's *logos,* or written revelation to His people, then you have no compass nor do you have a foundation or cornerstone in which to anchor to. You are advised by James (and the Holy Spirit) to find another vocation if you do not believe because you will be held accountable for every idle word that you utter.

Jesus did not mince any words when in Matthew 23:15, He said, *Woe to you, scribes and Pharisees, hypocrites! For you travel land*

and sea to win one proselyte, and when he is won, you make him twice as much a son of hell as yourselves. In fact, the entire chapter doesn't pull any punches. I am convinced that when Jesus said they made their converts "sons of hell", He was directly addressing the teachings of the Nicolaitans. One of the primary tactics that Satan has always used is to first cause God's creation to doubt His Word. The Nicolaitan spirit knows that if people begin to doubt, they become confused. If they are confused, they are vulnerable to a leader coming in and being their "savior". If there is no Truth that is available to everyone, then everyone must depend upon someone who has been decreed the conveyor of that Truth. That has been the case for centuries. Martin Luther and many like him, risked his life when he discovered that it was the will of God for everyone to possess that Truth. Luther called it the "priesthood of the believer". Just as the Nicolaitan spirit kicked in when Jesus healed the blind man on the Sabbath, it stirred up the leaders of the Catholic church who attempted to arrest and kill Luther. God, providentially, chose to protect Luther where he could finish the work that he began. Many other martyrs, however were killed for coming against this demonic stronghold. This spirit is no small force to be contended with. It will reach its highest peak when the "Great Harlot" in Rev.17 and the "False Prophet" in Rev.13 are revealed. Every false religious act and heresy will culminate at that time. That religious spirit will deceive many into taking the mark of the Beast in Rev.13, thinking they are serving God when they are actually giving homage to Satan.

The Nicolaitan Deception Is Taking Place Today

When I was attending the "Christian" college in the early 1970s (that taught that the Bible was not true), there were two extra-curricular religious groups that met. One was called the "Campus Congregation" and the one in which we met had no name. We found an empty classroom at night and met. The Campus Congregation had nice, religious meetings that were somewhat philosophical and serendipitous, but ultimately reinforced the idea that the Bible wasn't for today and that being nice and tolerant were all we needed.

On the other hand, our meetings consisted of people accepting Jesus Christ as their Savior, being filled with the Holy Spirit, people being healed, delivered from habits, sins, and demons, and gifts of the Spirit manifesting. Were all of our meetings perfect and without error? No, but God was there and we grew in Him and learned as all young Christians do.

The best analogy I can use to describe the difference between our meetings and the other ones would be to remember times when I was really hungry and would try to satisfy it with a candy bar or a bag of chips rather than a good meal. Their candy would give you a very momentary feeling of satisfaction, but would not genuinely give you the nutrition to cause you to grow or even remain alive. Paul referred to this as feeding the flock "milk" rather than "meat" in 1Corinthians 3 and Hebrews 5. In a similar way, Satan uses drugs (referred to as *sorcery, the Greek word being 'pharmakia', where we get pharmaceuticals*) to give someone a temporary feeling of euphoria to substitute in place of the genuine fulfillment of the Holy Spirit and God's kingdom.

The satisfaction from the religious spirit is limited to the brain and the emotions. God's presence affects our **spirit, soul, and body** (1 Thessalonians 5:23 and Hebrews 4:12). Man-made religion is limited to trying to understand God via the intellect, which we know is futile. The fulfillment of the *Holy Spirit* is brought about by God revealing Himself to us and dwelling within us. This is the "living water" Jesus was referring to in John 4 and 7. This living water is to be available to everyone, not just a chosen few. That was clearly exemplified by Jesus revealing it to the woman at the well whom everyone else, including herself, deemed unworthy.

The purpose of the Nicolaitan spirit today is to deceive people into believing in religion rather than God. It even goes further than that. It is a distraction to get people's eyes off of their only source of salvation and feel good about themselves, thus thinking that they are alright with God without having that personal relation-ship with Him. The Nicolaitan doctrine uses several methods previously mentioned such as believing that the pastor is the one who is the "professional Christian" who gets paid to walk closely with God. Therefore, we can go to this "mediator" and have him or her pray for us or counsel us and we have to go no further with our own responsibility to have that relationship with Jesus.

Another tactic that the Nicolaitan uses is to be that "mediator" to dissuade or discourage the believer into doubting the Word of God. This happens in those "cemeteries" called seminaries when they convince the ministerial candidates that the Bible is not true. Once fully brainwashed, the new minister goes and tries his/her best to subtly convince the congregation that God's Word is not true or only partially true. Once this works, even on a part of the congregation, it begins to spread like leaven in the whole loaf. Either the church becomes lukewarm, divided, or discouraged that they are having to deal with a pastor who does not believe.

I have dealt numerous times with churches that were in turmoil because a pastor "came out of the closet" and admitted that he or she did not truly believe. I have had pastors tell me that they did not believe in some of the basic premises of Christianity such as the virgin birth, the literal resurrection, the second coming and miracles. My question to them was, "Why are you in the ministry?" The sad news was that most of these ministers actually did truly believe and have a personal relationship with Jesus at one time. They were dissuaded from their faith in seminary or a similar setting.

Crack In the Windshield

I found that one of the most effective ways these people were deceived was what I call "the crack in the windshield method". I was sitting in a course of study class for training as part of our licensing process in my denomination. The professor was dynamic, devoted, gifted and very popular. I, and everyone else, was impressed by his teaching ability and by the way that he could inspire all of us. Then toward the end of the course, he very subtly inserted that he didn't believe in the inerrancy of the Bible and that we should include lifestyles in the church that the Bible clearly condemned. He did it so quickly that I caught myself considering if I was wrong since he and my peers seemed to agree. Then God showed me a "picture" of me driving my car down a road when a piece of gravel was thrown off of a dump truck and it hit my windshield and put a little crack in it. The crack looked harmless at first and was just a little annoying, but easy to ignore. Then days and weeks later, I noticed that the crack began to get bigger and longer, eventually ruining the whole windshield. That is how those subtle little rocks can shatter our faith unless we get rid of them from the beginning. There is a resin or glue that can prevent this crack in the windshield from spreading any further. The resin that can fix our windshield is the word "REPENTANCE". As soon as the Holy Spirit convicts us of an area of unbelief in our life, we can repent of it and not only is the windshield repaired, it is as if there never was a ding in it in the first place! That is the benefit of a personal relationship with Jesus. We do not have to go through another mediator or a ritual. We immediately have access to His throne of grace and forgiveness is instant.

Impure Motives

Another reason why people turn from their faith is that they do not have pure motives. I once was director of a drama ministry called the *Living Parables.* This ministry took the Gospel to thirty-six states, Jamaica and Mexico. Once the Holy Spirit gave me a word to the team that He would guarantee their success if they kept pure hearts, pure motives, and that they would stay humble before the Lord. Even though our particular ministry is no longer in existence, there is a lot of fruit still being borne as a result of it. There are people in the ministry and other drama ministries still going as a result of their fruit. Some left the ministry because they were looking at becoming a "star" and this ministry did not take them in that direction. God did not design us to be a star. There is only one Star, and that is the Morning Star Jesus (Rev. 22:16).

I know ministers who left their fundamental belief in the Word of God and began to preach that the Bible was not true. In every case, there was either something going on in their life that did not align with God's Word, or they had a beef with God over something in their life that did not go their way.

I got saved in 1971, filled with the Holy Spirit and accepted the call to preach in 1972. I have studied God's Word daily since that time. Each year that goes by, I am more convinced that everything in the Bible is true and has been or will be fulfilled. My experience with the Lord is personal, intimate, daily, and mutual. I talk to

God, and He talks to me. You cannot dissuade me from the belief in God nor His inspired Word because, as one minister put it, "the man with the experience, is not at the mercy of the man with the argument". I know other people in the ministry that have been in it longer than me who still are not only faithful, but are truly men of God who are spiritual "giants" in my eyes. They have pure hearts, pure motives and are humble in the sight of God. The problem of unbelief, of a hunger for power and control, of the Nicolaitan, is not a matter of the intellect, but of the heart. Unbelief, the fruit of the Nicolaitan spirit, is never of the Holy Spirit. Hebrews 4 says that unbelief will keep you out of the Kingdom (rest) of God.

Chapter 7

Nicolaitan Influence Counteracts True Fellowship

As I contrasted in the previous chapter the instance of the college prayer group verses "Campus Congregation", there is a difference between a religious meeting and divine fellowship. One may be the attempt to find or appease God and the other is simply to commune with Him and each other. Hebrews 10:24 says,

And let us consider one another to provoke unto love and to good works:²⁵ Not forsaking the assembling of ourselves together, as the manner

of some is; but exhorting one another: and so much the more, as ye see the day approaching.

When we come together, we are to strengthen, encourage, share burdens, and share what God has been doing in our lives. I have learned more from listening to people that I am ministering to, people that I have worked with, or just enjoyed the time with while having fun, than I have learned from any class. The true "seminary" is what I call the "seminary of life" (some call it the "school of hard knocks") where you share experiences with each other. This is where you allow the Holy Spirit to interact with each other and reveal Himself and his will to whoever is involved.

John Bunyan referred to the time of fellowship and encouragement as "discourse" in *Pilgrim's Progress*. Christian and Faithful would walk on the road to the Celestial City and talk of their own experiences and challenges, answering each other with Scripture. It said that they were having "discourse" with each other. It portrayed it as a major source of their strength. What if we had to wait upon the resident "expert" who was trained in such matters to help us? No, God wants us to understand that He wants us to have access directly to Him and we can strengthen and equip each other with the help of his Holy Spirit and his Word.

I love Billy Graham's quote: "If Christianity is true, it is not a religion." True Christianity is the whole body of Christ coming together and seeing each other as equal and valid parts of God's true church. It is *koinonia* or sharing life with each other.

I can visit another church of any denomination or "non-denomination" and within a few minutes feel the bond of the Holy Spirit formed by those who are there for the right reason. I believe that is what is truly meant by the term "kindred spirit". These people do not care what denomination you are affiliated with, they are just happy to fellowship with other believers. This is the true Church. I imagine that this is similar to what it will be like when we all meet in Heaven, many for the first time. I do not believe that there will be any strangers. Neither do I believe that there will be any cliques or elite groups. We will be one in Christ and He will exalt the humble and abase the haughty. These people are there to serve Jesus Christ, not their denomination.

As of the writing of this book, I am a pastor in the United Methodist Church. I will tell my peers or "superiors" that I do not work for our denomination; I work for Jesus Christ. I can find faults and areas in which I do not agree with the United Methodists, the Baptists, Pentecostals, Presbyterians, Episcopalians, Lutherans, Catholics, etc., whether they be formal, casual, liberal, conservative, traditional, or contemporary. Each have the influence of people's opinions and prejudices, yet each one also has a history of a genuine move of God that goes back to the beginnings of their group and is still a part of it.

Another characteristic each group (as a whole) has is that they have those believers who believe that they are there to serve God and share that fellowship and communion of the Holy Spirit. Some believe that denominations are not of God and others believe that non-denominational churches may be "of the devil". I have fellowshipped in both and served in both. I have found that they all have true believers and most of them have those who have not quiet "connected" yet. I believe that it is the will of God for us to come together in the unity of the faith (Eph. 4:13), and at that time, we will see true revival and perhaps the return of the Head of the Church, Jesus Christ himself.

That being said, I believe the purpose of Satan, through the Nicolaitan influence, is to prevent that revival from happening. If the people can feel unqualified or unworthy to serve God in the way He is calling them, there will not be the laborers for the harvest that Jesus referred to in Luke 10:2. We have prayer meeting one night a week. It is the least attended meeting that we have. I have seen the same phenomena in other churches that I attended or led. On the other hand, if you want a good turnout at a night meeting, have a hot topic that has to do with business or the building. Our priorities are the opposite of what Jesus was trying to get across. More than that, Satan is afraid of what will happen if we get together for prayer and spreading the Gospel. So the prayer meeting has two opponents that are impossible to over-come without yielding to the Spirit and the lord-ship of Christ in our lives. Those opponents are called the **flesh** and the **devil**. Ironically, the only way they can be overcome is by prayer. The Nicolaitan way of thinking reinforces the enemy with the attitude of "they are getting paid to do it", "I really don't know how to pray, I haven't been to seminary", "the church is only my business on Sunday", etc. Pastor Jim Cymbala (Author of *Fresh Wind, Fresh Fire*) said (my paraphrase) on Sunday morning you would find those who were faithful to the church, at Sunday night services you would find those who were faithful to the pastor, and at prayer meeting, you would find those where were serious about Jesus Christ. We learn to pray by praying. If we don't ever pray, we never learn. If we have someone who does all the praying for us, we will never have that blessed intimacy with God that He wants us to have. He wants our prayer experience to come boldly before the throne of Grace (Heb. 4:16) and boldly go where no man has ever gone before (Star Trek). That can only happen if we realize that God has provided that free access to **all** who believe, not just a few.

NICOLAITAN STRATEGIES IN DIFFERENT SETTINGS

Each church group or denomination is susceptible to the influence of the Nicolaitan spirit. The one that has the oldest tradition of the priesthood being separate from the clergy is the Roman Catholic Church. Many people like to blame all the ills of the modern church on the actions that took place in the Roman Catholic Church, but I want to emphasize, it is not the Catholic Church that is the enemy, but the Nicolaitan spirit that took a stronghold in the early church that developed into that mindset. Let's look at several different groups, one-by-one and see the different ways that spirit operates. In the next chapter, we will look at the way or ways to overcome it.

CATHOLIC AND ORTHODOX CHURCHES

The Roman Catholic church preaches that they are the original and "true" Church that started with Peter when Jesus told him that "… upon this rock, I will build my church" (Matthew 16:18). We discussed earlier how that Jesus did not mean upon Peter, but upon the confession that Jesus Christ is the Messiah, the Son of the Living God. This idea was not a simple mistake on their part, but an intentional twist of the meaning of the Scripture to implement a position of power that had ultimate authority in the Church. Over the years, popes used and misused this power for political and financial purposes that were anything but godly. Doctrines that resulted in the worship of Mary and the apostles, Purgatory, Indulgences, worship of angels, worship of relics, the inquisition, the Crusades, the killing of innocent people in the name of God, and many others were all

121

created by men who had ultimate and unchallenged authority. They even had the authority to change Scripture if they wished.

By now, those who did such things understand the meaning of Rev. 22 that says: *I testify to everyone who hears the words of the prophecy of this book: if anyone adds to them, God will add to him the plagues which are written in this book; [19] and if anyone takes away from the words of the book of this prophecy, God will take away his part from the tree of life and from the holy city, which are written in this book.* What they did not believe while they lived on earth, they most certainly believe now.

The obvious question is, how did the early Church slip into that kind of thinking? Jesus answered it in his warning to the churches of Ephesus and Pergamum in chapter 2. Let's look at the way the admonition is phrased in verses 14-15.

...[14] *But I have a few things against you,
because you have there those who hold the doctrine of Balaam, who taught Balak to put a stumbling block before the children of Israel, to eat
things sacrificed to idols, and to commit sexual
immorality.* [15] *Thus you also have those who hold
the doctrine of the Nicolaitans, which thing I hate.*

The word, "thus" in verse 15 seems to show
a connection between "those who hold the doctrine of Balaam" and those who also have the
doctrine of the Nicolaitans. I do not believe that
this is showing a similarity in the doctrine, but a
similarity of the person's authority or power to
create such a doctrine. The Nicolaitan would
have an impression of authority that the people
would believe in and fear. That would give them
the ability to create doctrine that went against
Scripture without opposition. Thus the reason
the enemy put the Nicolaitans in the Church;
to produce false doctrine that usurps the
authority of Jesus and takes away the ability

of the believer to have that direct connection to their Lord and Savior. So in all earnest, corrupt people who were not serving Jesus Christ slipped into a position of authority and steered the Church into the wrong direction. Because of fear and a willingness to compromise and keep silent, the true Church allowed it or they were persecuted for it. This transition was slow and subtle (sound familiar?) like the illustration of dropping a frog into lukewarm water until it reached the boiling point and the frog never noticed until it was too late.

Therefore, the Roman Catholic Church accepts these false doctrines as traditions and sees them as a type of "evolution" of the church that brought them to where they are today. The problem with that is, it has brought them farther away. How often do we hear of people knowingly committing sins or even heinous crimes, knowing that they are going to do them again, yet they will go and confess to the priest (who is their "mediator") and have their sins resolved after performing some unscriptural "penance" that has nothing to do with the cleansing Blood of Jesus?

SACRAMENTS

I am about to say something here that some will call "blasphemous". The use of sacraments was created by the Nicolaitans as a tool to cause that dividing-line between clergy and laity. Use any Bible search tool or concordance. You will not find it in the Bible. Merriam-Webster calls "sacraments": "a Christian rite (as baptism or the Eucharist) that is believed to have been ordained by Christ and that is held to be a means of divine grace or to be a sign or symbol of a spiritual reality." *Theopedia* adds that it is "a visible sign of Grace." There is nothing wrong with believing in a sacrament in that context. What is wrong, is believing that

God only made the handling or performing of the sacraments available to people who jumped through man-made "hoops". The Old Testament priests were the only ones who could go into the Holy of Holies and stand before the Ark of the Covenant to sprinkle the blood of the lamb on the altar. Anyone else would automatically die. That priest would have to be recognized as ordained by God, from the right bloodline, having gone through the right training and cleansing rituals before he could stand before the altar of God. In the New Testament, it was made clear that JESUS is our high priest and became all of those sacraments for us. He gave us direct access to Him and called us **all** to be priests and kings. To say that anyone has more access to the things of the Kingdom of God is to say that Jesus has not done it all. The one sacrament that He gave to all of us to connect to Him is called *faith.* The way to connect directly to Him is to *believe.* John 1:12 says, *But, as* *many as received Him, to them He gave the right to become children of God, to those who believe in His name.*

Although we are all called to confess our sins to one another and forgive each other (James 5:16), God meant for all of us to do it; not just a chosen few. What qualifies these priests to do this? After going through years of study of their doctrine and practices and acts of service that are observed by their "superiors", they are finally awarded the ordination required to administer the Sacraments and to preach the Word and forgive sins. The hours of study and work are so arduous and difficult that finally reaching the status of being called "reverend", "priest", "father", "monsignor", "friar", etc., makes one feel as if the titles are truly earned and deserved. I feel that this is ironic and tragic. God has ordained all of the Body of Christ and called all of into that ministry of reconciliation. Yes, He has called us to be apostles, prophets, evangelists, pastors and teachers (Eph. 4). He has also given us more callings and ministries throughout the New Testament (see Romans 12, 1 Corinthians 12-14 and Acts). The difference is, it is not man who can ordain and call us, it is God. God called us to be servants, not lords. He called us to humble ourselves, not to seek to be exalted by others. True ordination comes from God and will be recognized by the Church. If it has to be forced upon the people to believe it, it is not from God.

"MAINSTREAM CHURCHES"

I was recently in a class where the professor was discussing what the largest Protestant "mainstream churches" were. When he didn't mention Baptist, many were shocked. He let us know that the Baptists were not considered "mainstream". He was implying that those Protestant churches that still held to some of the traditions that were residual from the Catholic Church were to be taken as "real" churches. It was also implying that everyone from the Baptists to the Charismatics were not to be given the credence that the "mainstream churches" were. The irony in that is that the Catholic and Orthodox churches think the same of the Episcopals, Methodists, Lutherans, Presbyterians, as these denominations think of the non "mainstream" Baptists and others. Notice that the more formal and "liturgized" a church is, the more the world seems to tolerate it? That is because the world is not challenged by something they do not take seriously. Performing a few rituals and ceremonies are surely not harmful if that is what someone wants to do to feel more comfortable with their religion so long as it does not challenge the way a person lives nor cause them to want to change.

I can say that the United Methodists of today as well as the Episcopalians (from whence the

Methodists came), have a more difficult means of arriving at "ordination" than the Baptists do. I am all for background checks, psychological exams, training in leadership, study, classes on the Bible and ministry, etc. But when I hear the professors teaching a "tongue in cheek" approach to the Bible as if it is an outdated book of myths and the students buy into that idea, then teach it to the churches, then I see where unbelief has replaced faith and hope is replaced with despair and depression. The United Methodists require that we listen to these classes on theology which started out as a good thing, but slowly were replaced with "Heresy 101". Now many of the theology classes are provided with pseudo-intellectual approaches to God and the Bible that are merely excuses to doubt and not believe at all. The outcome of this is, if none of it is true, then I can live any way I want to and do whatever I want. My question is, if you don't believe any of it, why aren't you in another line of work? **Do you feel a calling from God to turn people away from the faith?** You need to consider who you are really working for. Of course you don't really believe that the devil exists, so again I ask, why are you doing it?

The real reason people get caught up into this is not that they set out to do so. Most that I know started out with a genuine, sincere, child-like faith; felt the call to the ministry, and did what they felt they were supposed to do and began with college, then going to seminary. The process began with what I call "hoop-jumping" and that continued throughout the process. The farther into the process you went, the more and difficult the "hoops" became. The classes got harder, the papers got longer, the time spent in actual ministry as a student-pastor or youth worker became more like part of the class rather than genuine ministry. You were told that you were different from the regular "lay-person" and you were to form "professional boundaries" between you and them (you don't want to get too close, you might get hurt). Soon this glorious ministry you envisioned became a career, ministry became a "job" and you had jumped through too many "hoops" to turn back. Your only recourse was to follow through and accept that really was what God called you to do (if God really did things like that).

I warned some young people who were going into the ministry about what they would try to teach them in seminary (I even called it "cemetery" like my Uncle Thornton did.) They assured me that they would stay faithful and would keep believing the Bible and stay in prayer. By the time some of them got out, they did not believe anymore. One even professed to be an agnostic. What happened? They found a professor or professors who were genuinely gifted teachers in whom they put all of their trust. These professors had a hidden agenda and by the time these students graduated, they became followers of the professors (who were false teachers that Jesus and the epistles warned about; dressed in sheep's clothing).

What causes the teachers to teach false doctrine? Well the simple answer is, Satan. The more complex answer is that if they started out as sincere, they left a "chink" in their armor such as pride, desire for recognition or power or something similar. Another reason is that they just have a "beef" with God. After some bad encounters with some of these disciples of doubt, I heard some of their life stories. One had a wife that left him unexpectedly and he decided that God had abandoned him or He did not exist at all. Another had another sort of tragedy that he was mad at God about. Yet, another was living in an adulterous affair and others in life-styles that they knew would not coincide with teaching the Scripture in a sincere way. When this is going on, you either have to back away from teaching the Gospel or find a way to make it fit your lifestyle to where guilt or conviction won't overwhelm you. There is no set way the enemy will try to turn us from our faith. He will focus on any weakness that you may have. Our only way to defend is to stay in constant communion with God through Jesus by the power of the Holy Spirit.

I digress, but I feel it was necessary. The way the Nicolaitans get into the "mainstream" churches is through focusing on man-made liturgy rather than helping individuals to become followers and ministers of Christ. Learning to use theological sesquipedalian terms (long words), and developing a religious "shop talk" that only peers can understand, causes the "lay person" to feel as if they are underqualified to converse with the "clergy". These theological terms are not godly means of edifying or equipping the saints. They are means of providing an illusion of superiority of the clergyman and a feeling of insecurity and unworthiness with the layperson. Jesus hates this because it hinders the growth of the young Christian and creates a feeling of inadequacy in that person. The way we grow in Christ is to have complete access and constant communication with Him.

The Lutherans broke away from the Roman church when Martin Luther recognized the hypocrisy and ungodly control from the church. He was nearly executed for it. The Nicolaitans tried to kill him for simply recognizing that we were saved by grace and it was not by works. Luther preached fervently about the priesthood of the believer and that every believer had direct access to God through Jesus Christ. Sadly, as the years passed, his followers started slipping back into the ritualistic clergy-laity type of thinking.

The Methodists had more subtly moved away from the Church of England and their logistics of winning souls and preaching in the missionary setting of America forced them to rely on "lay preachers" or "exhorters" to preach the Gospel in the new frontier. Although, Wesley wanted to go by the rules of the Episcopal Church for ordination, etc., the difficulty of preaching by commuting from church to church on horseback over long distances forced them to rely upon preachers who had not gone through all the "hoops" to pastor and administer the sacraments. The Presiding Elder, Frances Asbury, became "Bishop Asbury" to the Americans after he was very successful in enabling many men of God to go throughout the frontier churches and preach the Gospel. Preachers like Peter Cartwright were little more than lay-speakers, yet won hundreds and thousands of souls to Christ.

In the early 60's, the Methodist Church combined with the Evangelical United Brethren ,who were more evangelical than the Methodists at that time, and became the United Methodists. Before and during that time, they would, like a pendulum, go from becoming more liturgical and formal to more casual and informal. They experienced an emphasis on education and intellectualism in the 50s and 60s, and the numbers began to wane. Then there was the the Lay-Witness Movement, Charismatic Movement, "Walk to Emmaus" Movement, and other movements in the 70s through the 90s where many began to grow again. Large congregations like Frazier Memorial in Birmingham had lively, contemporary Spirit-led worship and the church was packed out in the thousands for several services. This growth happened because there was an emphasis on the truth of the Gospel and liberty to let the Holy Spirit move.

Now there is a move to try to bring the church back to a traditional "Wesleyanism" which is in actuality, far from what John Wesley lived or preached. It is more like what Jesus called "straining at gnats and swallowing camels" (Matt.23:24). One such example is that of a pastor friend of mine who was preaching the Gospel under such anointing that many of the church members were being born-again and seeking to be baptized. We had dozens of baptisms over a short period of time. It was discovered that some of the new converts had been baptized as infants. This second baptism actually had Scriptural precedent as is found in Acts 19 when Paul found some disciples who had been baptized with John's baptism. Then Paul prayed with them to be baptized with the Holy Spirit. Next, they baptized them in the "name of the Lord Jesus" (verse 5). Because the United Methodists still hold to the doctrine of infant baptism (passed down from the Roman Catholics, then to the Church of England) and it is against their discipline to baptize a second time, this pastor was reprimanded and disciplined. There was no mention of rejoicing that many people had been saved from Hell and made citizens of the Kingdom of God, just swift and sure punishment for overlooking some of the man-made rules. Sound familiar? Like when Jesus was rebuked for healing on the Sabbath? They sure got all of the "gnats" strained out though. This is an example of wielding the sword of "authority" rather than the Sword of the Spirit (Eph. 6). It was an act of the Nicolaitan spirit.

The clergy-laity system in the United Methodist Church draws a wide distinctive line between "ordained" and "non-ordained" members. Lay-speakers, lay-servants, and licensed local pastors may preach and lead local congregations. The lay ministers may not serve communion or baptize, but the licensed local pastors may in their local church. Ordained elders and deacons may perform these ceremonies in any church, they have more voting privileges in Annual Conference, get appointed to larger churches and have more benefits. These positions are earned by going to seminary, much work, scrutiny, practice, and many other difficult tasks. Attaining the status of ordination is so difficult that it creates a feeling of having earned it through hard work and sacrifice. It also creates animosity between those serving as ordained and non-ordained. The ordained feel that those who are not, do not deserve the privileges because they did not earn it. The non-ordained, some of whom have done as much work and study, often feel "inferior" to the ordained. The problem with the entire premise is that it is based upon theological training and practices that are now made by people rather than created by God. Theological training consists of classes that teach that the Bible is not completely true and approaches it from a totally intellectual, what I call "two-dimensional", approach. The dimension of the Holy Spirit revealing and interpreting Scripture is left out because of unbelief. Many practice and believe that the ministry is a career, not a calling. Much of the motivation today is based upon what it will take to get the bigger church with the larger salary or a position of recognition and power.

This is a vast contrast to the early Methodist Church when circuit riders would go from church to church through rough and dangerous country and bad weather because they felt called to preach the Gospel. During the frontier times, the average life span of a Methodist circuit-riding preacher was less than 40 years old. Many died from disease, weather, animal attacks, and sometimes hostile locals. These people also studied and worked hard to obtain their ministry. However, they believed that the Holy Scriptures were really Holy. They believed what the Bible taught was true, and they gave their lives for it. What happened to move that denomination to a Laodicean lifestyle? It was impure motives and hearts that were darkened by the deeds of the Nicolaitans.

AUTONOMOUS AND INDEPENDENT CHURCHES

The Baptists were looked down upon by the "mainstream" denominations. They pulled away from the Nicolaitan doctrines and practices and set up local church systems where the pastor was ordained and recognized by other ordained ministers, elders, deacons, and the local congregation. When you say the word "Baptist" though, you can be talking about a number of different approaches to beliefs as well as church governments. Just a limited list of the main headings of the different types of Baptists in the United States numbers over sixty. That is not to mention the independent congregations that come under no group covering. There are Bible Baptists, General Baptists, Freewill Baptists, Primitive Baptists, Missionary Baptists, Southern Baptists, Northern Baptists, Alliance Baptists, Separate Baptists in Christ, United

Baptists, Full-Gospel Baptists, Unregistered Baptists (I guess they're registered now to have a title), and many, many more. The one thing that most of these Baptists have in common is that they are "autonomous". They do not have to submit to a ruling body to function. This was probably a very good attempt to break away from the Nicolaitan spirit and doctrine, however it just set them up for a different twist.

The Baptists, other independent churches, and non-denominational churches have a whole new set of problems from the Nicolaitan spirit. The pastor, elders, deacons can be set up as the mediators between God and the congregants. It is actually much easier to have the ruler-subservient relationship without any outsiders to help safeguard against it. I have watched churches ranging from Baptist to Charismatic have a virtual tyrant running things. I have seen meetings where the pastor would literally scream at the elders and deacons if things were not going as he thought they were supposed to. I have seen congregations emulate the pastor's mannerisms, dress, lifestyle, etc. out of adoration for that individual or group, forgetting that they were to be emulating and following Jesus, not that pastor. I have seen people in a church literally fear the wrath of that pastor or staff to the point of feeling pressure to even lie to escape the wrath and reprimands of those leaders. This is how cults start. This is another work of the Nicolaitan spirit. That same spirit caused the Jim Jones, David Koresh, and myriads of other less-known cults that were formed in the name of Jesus Christ. Soon, the name of Jesus was not mentioned much, but the name of the leader was mentioned in every conversation. That individual or group became the "priest". The followers of Jim Jones favorite quote was, "we have a god that we can see and touch".

In the 70s and 80s, there was a popular teaching out in the Charismatic groups called the "Shepherding Movement". This taught that everyone should have a "covering" and you should "submit" to elders or pastors to stay safe from the attacks of the devil and from the world. One such ministry was prevalent among college campuses. In college in the early 70s, I was told many times that I was not "in submission" or not "under a covering" because I was not in their particular fellowship. I was also told that I was in "their territory" and was "out of God's will" because I didn't "submit" what I was doing to their leadership. What made it worse was that my girlfriend, at that time, was originally a member of their group and she didn't ask them if she could be with me. I simply ignored them and avoided them. Today, the group doesn't exist and many who were in it are still serving God, but learned a lesson the hard way while staying in that group. Others left the group and left their Christian walk with it. The reason is that they were totally dependent upon the leader rather than being taught to depend upon Jesus.

Many Christians were hurt as a result of that movement and false doctrine that was a result of it. They were more casualties caused by the deeds of the Nicolaitans. Many of these fellowships started with sincere people, sincerely trying to serve God in a pure way, but the enemy sneaks in to steal, kill, and destroy. I cannot emphasize enough, pure hearts, pure motives, and staying real and humble before the Lord is the best safeguard against this spirit. Self-examination on a daily basis will ensure that you can avoid drifting into this mentality. Psalm 139:23, *Search me, O God, and know my heart; Try me, and know my anxieties*; is asking the Holy Spirit to turn on his "searchlight" within our hearts every day. That is what will keep us fixed upon Him.

Chapter 8

HOW, THEN, SHOULD IT BE DONE?

This book is not intended to be an expose' or to construct a conspiracy theory. It is merely to show a problem that has been in the Church for centuries and ways to make it right. The way God's grace works is to take our imperfections, faults, and sins away and redirect us back onto the path to God's perfection.

Some accept the way the Church functions now and believe that it has simply "evolved" into what it is today. They believe that the age of reason has merged man's intellect with a measure of faith and reached a great compromise between what we experience with our five senses and what lies beyond those senses in a realm that we call "spiritual". As long as we do not take this "spiritual" realm too seriously so as to contradict our realm of "reason", we can pretend to have faith in something as long as we are guided by "trained professionals" who know how to use theology as a tool to smooth over pure unbelief. That way, we can focus our efforts upon anything we want to and not have to waste our time on "spiritual things".

My point is, what if the entire Body of Christ, which we call the Church, was intent upon spending all of its effort doing what God called us to do? What if we were fulfilling our calling and using the individual gifts that God gave us to spread the Kingdom of God? If we could recognize the true calling and potential that was given to us, we could be world changers. If we took prayer seriously as our first priority, instead of letting a "priest" or "clergyperson" do it for us, we would have dozens or hundreds of people praying instead of one.

A wonderful example is that of an Englishman, Reece Howells, who lived near the turn of the 19th into the 20th century. He discovered the power of prayer as he spent most of his time walking (not driving) from place to place praying. The more time he spent in prayer, the more prayers got answered. Lives changed, souls were saved, miracles and healings occurred. People that he influenced began to join him in prayer. Bigger and more far-reaching miracles happened and prayer groups formed all over England. These prayers changed the course of world history. In World War II, some of Hitler's blunders were connected directly to prayers that were specifically prayed by Howell's prayer groups. They prayed that Germany would not invade England during the war and, inexplicably, Hitler only sent the bombers thinking that would be enough to win. It is said that if

Hitler had followed the bombing with an invasion, he would have certainly defeated England. Howell's group also prayed for Hitler to be confused and make wrong decisions later in the war when he decided to invade Russia in the winter, splitting and weakening his forces, thus being stopped by the Russians. One more thing that his prayer groups did that changed history, to the point of fulfilling Bible prophecy, happened in 1947. Howell's prayer groups prayed for the nation of Israel to be reborn. No one thought that was even a remote possibility. On May 14th, 1948, the League of Nations voted to recognize the nation of Israel in the land of Palestine. With opposition from all the Arab nations and many others, Israel was reborn in one day, thus fulfilling important end-times Bible prophecy.

What is the point of all this? It shows what can happen when the Body of Christ can function as He willed it to be without being restrained by bureaucracy and unbelief. Prayer is just in one area. What would happen if everyone had a vision of what God could do through them? The enemy has convinced God's people that we are "unqualified", so we should not do anything for the Kingdom of God. What if people who had the "gift of gab" and were great salesmen, teachers, support-people, etc., believed that their first and foremost reason for having that gift was to win other people to Christ? If artists, builders, engineers, writers, musicians, those gifted in finances, cooks, managers, coaches, on and on, utilized their God-given gifts toward God's purpose without restraint, there would be no struggling congregations and the majority of people would not be lost in the world today.

There is still hope as well as time if we as believers can do as Jesus told us to do in Revelation 2:16. The word was, *Repent, or else I will come to you quickly and will fight against them with the sword of My mouth.* After each admonishment in Revelation 2 and 3, Jesus said, "repent". To do so, we need to turn toward the Scripture to see how to work in the ministry that God has given us, and turn away from man's tradition that has been infiltrated by the doctrines of the Nicolaitans. Yes, we need to **repent** and listen to what the Spirit says to churches today. I am not advocating pulling out of our present setting or denomination and starting a new one. That is what happened throughout the ages and kept turning into new denominations. We need to repent of that place in which we lost our "first love" as the church of Ephesus did in Rev. 2:4. That repentance would require forgetting focusing on the man-made rules and regulations that distract us from that great love that we experienced when we met Christ for the first time. He would have us return to that child-like faith and say, "Father, what would you have me do?"

Ephesians 4:11 says, *And He Himself gave some to be apostles, some prophets, some* *evangelists, and some pastors, and teachers,* *12 **for the equipping of the saints for the work of ministry, for the edifying of the body of Christ**. There is a popular teaching that has much merit called the "Five-fold Ministry" teaching which is connected to this Scripture. I agree with much of it, however some treat it as if these are the only five ministries that have credence. I Corinthians 12:27 says, *Now, you are the body of Christ, and members individually.* *28 And God has appointed these in the church: first apostles, second prophets, third teachers, after that miracles, then gifts of healings, helps, administrations, varieties of tongues.* Notice how it mentions some of the same gifts as Ephesians 4 with the addition of some more. Then there are the ministry gifts mentioned in Romans 12. It says, beginning in verse 6, *Having then gifts differing according to the grace that is given to us, let us use them: if prophecy, let us prophesy in proportion to our* *faith; [7] or ministry, let us use it in our ministering; he who teaches, in teaching; [8] he who exhorts, in exhortation; he who gives, with liberality; he who leads, with diligence; he who shows mercy, with cheerfulness.*

I believe that these are also not all-inclusive. There are many music and worship-leading related gifts that are either not mentioned or could come under some sub-category of *ministry* or *exhortation.* Usually, the first thing I think of when I hear the word "exhortation" is someone correcting me about some error in my life. The word in the Scripture used for exhortation literally means "encouragement". It might be to encourage after a failure, or just encouragement to continue what God is doing through you right now. That can easily be done with worship music, preaching, and other similar forms of ministry.

There are many other types of caring, leadership, provision, discerning, wisdom, even technological gifts, that it is obvious that God has given yet they are not all mentioned for the simple reason, you could have an endless list of them. Also, we are not limited to just one gift or ability. Remember the parable of the talents in Matthew 25? One had five, one had two, and one had only one. I fully believe that this parable is directly connected to the gifts that God has given us. Do you remember the fate of the person who only had one and went and hid it? He ended up weeping and gnashing his teeth. **Do you see what the Nicolaitan error has caused here? Multitudes of people are burying their talents and others are attempting to do things that have nothing to do with their individual gifts.**

What is the church, across the board, lacking? People are not using the talents that God has given them. They are either not using them at all, or they are not using them for the glory of God; they are using them for themselves. Listen, you are responsible for hearing God and knowing what his calling is for your life. It is perfectly ok and even expected for others of God's people to help us do that. That is why he mentioned many of these ministry gifts.

Chapter 9

MINISTRY GIFTS

Apostles

L et's look at a few of these from Ephesians 4. "First apostles". The word for apostle simply means "sent one". Another Nicolaitan teaching says that they are elevated above all others and that they had to be one of the original disciples who walked with Jesus. Paul is proof that it does not have to be one of the "originals". The only thing I agree with there is that the apostle has to "walk with Jesus", but that even includes today. **The elevation of the title, "apostle", to**

a place that seems unattainable, is another attempt by the Nicolaitan spirit to prevent the body of Christ from fulfilling its calling. The flip-side of that elevated status is also seen when some present-day individuals have been called "apostle" and it elevated their ego. I once knew a man who handed out business cards with his name followed by the title, "Apostle". I would imagine that most of his cards wound up in the trash. This calling is a ministry, a recognition of abilities and gifts; **it is not a title**. I believe that people who obeyed God, and God started a great work through them, can be classified as "apostles" but they would never have let anyone call them that. Some examples are men such as St. Patrick, the Irish monk, Aiden (who introduced Christianity to the Vikings), Judson in China, Livingstone in Africa, Martin Luther, John Wesley and myriads of others. They established a base for people to plant their feet on and begin the work of God in a certain area. These "apostles" obviously had other gifts and talents mentioned in Ephesians 4 to fulfill their mission.

Prophets

The next ministry mentioned is that of "prophet". The word prophet refers to a vessel who God speaks through. Often, the first image to come to mind is of a person in a long robe and beard with a staff in their hand resembling Gandalf from *Lord of the Rings*. I have heard prophetic utterances and spoken them myself. Many have started with "thus saith the Lord" to get the listener's attention, however that is not necessary. I have had people make a statement to me in a casual tone of voice that changed my life because the Holy Spirit was speaking directly through them. We all have the ability for God to use us as a vessel by His Spirit speaking through us. The prophetic Word needs to be spoken to the Church regularly, whether in a sermon, a lesson, or a direct statement. It is the living Word of God that empowers and feeds his people. People wonder why fewer people are going to church. It is because believers come to fellowship to be fed the Living Bread, to hear the Word of God, and to be transformed into His image. Christians need the prophet to be functioning in God's Church today as much as ever in history.

Evangelists

When I first got saved, I thought I should try to look and dress like the evangelist who was preaching when I received Jesus into my heart. I also remember wanting to emulate Billy Graham (I am still one of his biggest fans. I believe when he dies, it may trigger the rapture.) I soon realized that God did not want me to be one of them. He wanted me to be me, full of the Holy Spirit. We all have a call to evangelize and make disciples (Mark 16:15, Matthew 28:18, 2 Corinthians 5:18, etc.). We have all been given the job of winning souls, but there are some who obviously have a special calling to do so. I have one friend, Bro. Harold Witmer, who cannot have a conversation without talking about Jesus. Over the years, I have seen him lead more people to the Lord than anyone I know by simply having Jesus as the center of his life and being confident that God is going to speak through him with the words that he needs to lead people to Jesus daily. You can read about him in his biography called *Brother Harold*, by Joe Garner Turman, printed by Truth Book Publishers. Harold has the ministry of an evangelist, but as I said, God speaks through him, therefore he also has the ability of a prophet. He has established multiple ministries, thus also having some of the same gifts as an apostle, but I think all who know him would agree that his main calling is that of an evangelist.

I was recently doing one of my prayer walks and was worshiping the Lord and I began to feel the moving of the Holy Spirit within me. Not only was I feeling the joy, peace, and love that comes with that experience, but I felt that love reaching out and I was wanting to tell people about Jesus and his salvation. It then registered to me that when we are full of the Holy Spirit, and He permeates our very DNA molecules, He is downloading the Heart of God into us. God's desire is for us to tell everyone about His love and salvation. When we are full of his Spirit, that also becomes our desire. Do you have a hard time expressing yourself when you try to witness to someone? Pray and seek God and be filled with the Holy Spirit and evangelism will be a natural thing that comes out of your mouth, not a thing that we do out of duty or guilt. **Evangelism is a gift** that God gives to everyone. **The ministry of an Evangelist** is a special calling that God gives to whom He chooses.

Pastors

The word "pastor" comes from the same root word as "shepherd" where we even get the word "pasture". As I mentioned earlier, a pastor is not like the butcher that drives the sheep, but he is the one who leads. A New Testament shepherd is simply a follower of the "Chief Shepherd" who has the assignment of leading the other sheep toward him. It would be more accurate to view him as the sheep who keeps the other sheep looking at the Chief Shepherd.

1 Peter 5 says it like this:

1 The elders who are among you I exhort, I who am a fellow elder and a witness of the sufferings of Christ, and also a partaker of the glory that will be revealed: 2 Shepherd the flock

*of God which is among you, serving as over-
seers, not by compulsion but willingly, not for
dishonest gain but eagerly; ³ nor as being lords
over those entrusted to you, but being examples to the flock; ⁴ and when the Chief Shepherd
appears, you will receive the crown of glory that
does not fade away.*

See how Peter called himself a "fellow elder"
(not "Pope Peter")? He addressed the other
elders or shepherds as equals and referred to
them as "overseers, not by compulsion but willingly…". He is saying "we're all in this together
following Christ." I would definitely want to hear
from someone who walked with Jesus for three
and a half years and witnessed his sufferings
and resurrection, but again I say that Jesus
chose him and all the rest because they were
people like you and me. This humility and willingness to "keep it real" pertaining to who he
really was, and was not, is why Peter was able
to follow Jesus all the way to the upside down

cross that he was crucified on. There is no way Peter could have done that without the help of Jesus and he could not have received that kind of help without walking in that kind of humility.

Ezekiel 34, which was mentioned earlier in the book, talks about another type of shepherd who is not really a shepherd at all. Their actions, or lack thereof, become the prophetic reason that the Chief Shepherd comes to change their system. This Scripture describes the actions and attitudes of the Nicolaitans to a tee.

The Shepherds had become butchers. The sheep had become people who were "devoured" by following through fear and intimidation. Rather than the elders being servants, they were rulers and the sheep were their slaves; thus fulfilling the definition of the Nicolaitan. God is calling shepherds who are like the Chief Shepherd *who humbled Himself and became obedient to the point of death, even the death of the cross.* (Philippians 2:8). Jesus regularly referred to Himself as a servant and to his followers as servants.

A true shepherd of God should never seek to be served, but should have the heart of a servant.

The ministry of the pastor is a true calling of God but it is not as a mediator between the people and God. They only have one Mediator, that is Christ Jesus. The pastor's role is simply one who has spiritual maturity (elder) and helps the other sheep on their journey to the Kingdom of God. Paul said in Philippians 3:17, *Brethren, join in following my example, and note those who so walk, as you have us for a pattern.* Paul did not say to follow him, but to follow his example. Pastors are to pray and seek God and keep the flock from straying from the Scripture and the grace of God. They are to be on watch for wolves in sheep's clothing and for those who cause dissention. **Pastors who fell asleep during their watch are the ones who let the spirit of the Nicolaitans creep into the Church or to their own motives.** They were not doing the job of a pastor. When the pastor lets the enemy creep into their heart and change their motives, they switch over to the "dark side" as it is referred to in *Star Wars,* and they become a wolf. Just as Jesus forgave his disciples when they fell asleep while He was in Gethsemane, in Revelation 2, Jesus offered an opportunity for those who had done so to come back by repenting of that as the sin that it is. Jesus does not want any more wolves tending his flock. He said that He would come and be our own personal Shepherd. The last verse of the section in Ezekiel 34 says it like this:

31 You are My flock, the flock of My pasture; you are men, and I am your God," says the Lord GOD.

The role of the pastor is to lead and teach God's people how to allow Jesus to be their own personal Shepherd. It is **not** to be the mediator between the flock and God. When this occurs, we will have a powerful and faithful army that will result in a powerful and world-wide revival. Millions of souls will be brought to Christ and the great harvest will occur. It will be a manifestation of the Holy Spirit being poured out upon the whole Body of Christ, young and old, rich and poor, people of all types. It will look like the description taken from Peter's sermon in Acts 2 and Joel 2 which says:

'And it shall come to pass in the last days, says God,
That I will pour out of My Spirit on all flesh;
Your sons and your daughters shall prophesy,
Your young men shall see visions,
Your old men shall dream dreams.

¹⁸ And on My menservants and on My maidservants

I will pour out My Spirit in those days;

And they shall prophesy.

¹⁹ I will show wonders in heaven above

And signs in the earth beneath:

Blood and fire and vapor of smoke.

²⁰ The sun shall be turned into darkness,

And the moon into blood,

*Before the coming of the great and awesome day of the L*ORD*.*

²¹ And it shall come to pass

That whoever calls on the name of the LORD **Shall be saved.**

This will not happen as a result of televangelists or speakers with large arenas and followings. It will be a result of the entire Body of Christ realizing that each individual is an important part of what God is doing and that each one of us is just as vital to God as the next. Body of Christ, stop depending upon your pastor to do your part for you! It can only be done by you.

TEACHERS

The "Teaching Movement" became popular in the '70s and grew more and more effective since that time. Now Christians are getting fed through videos and downloads in every kind of media imaginable. As Jesus forecasted in Matthew 24, Luke 21 and several other places though, there are also many false teachers out there too.

Some of the false teachings included the "Shepherding Movement" that literally established a priesthood or mediator over laity by forcing the Church to submit to an "elder or shepherd". There was the "Prosperity Movement" that caused the Christian to focus upon themselves, using the promises of God found in the Bible to satisfy selfish wants and needs. There are now many teachings that emphasize grace to the extent that anyone can do whatever they want to without regard to God or man and "grace will cover it all." This unbalanced teaching takes away all responsibility to fellow Christians and any need for discipleship.

(**Matthew 5:19-** *Whoever therefore breaks one of the least of these commandments, and teaches men so, shall be called least in the kingdom of heaven; but whoever does and teaches them, he shall be called great in the kingdom of heaven.)*

I realize that everything we do is a result of God's Grace, but that also includes being one of his disciples and experiencing *sanctification, holiness, and obedience,* thus fulfilling God's calling upon one's life.

Other false teachings over the years that are just as destructive to Christianity are those that embrace *legalism*. Just as the unbalanced grace teaching teaches something other than the Christian walk, the legalistic approach takes away our ability to follow Jesus by placing the task in our own hands and out of the Holy Spirit's. I have seen churches who emphasized what kind of clothes and makeup to wear or not to wear, yet they were quick to indulge in sexual immorality, gluttony, gossip and mistreating others. This type of legalism has a form of godliness, but it is only on the surface, not in the heart. All of these teachings and many more are tactics that the devil uses to keep the church distracted and missing its true purpose.

God needs true teachers of his Word to teach the Body of Christ to follow Jesus and have a personal relationship with Him. He needs teachers who are humble and dependent upon his Spirit to rightly divide the Word of Truth and present it to the Church. He does not need "experts" who draw attention to themselves and off of Jesus, nor does He need those who want to even share the glory with Jesus. Teachers, learn to depend upon the Holy Spirit to help you to understand, interpret, and deliver the Word of God. Luke 12:11-12 says: *¹¹ Now when they bring you to the synagogues and magistrates and authorities, do not worry about how or what you should answer, or what you should say. ¹² For the Holy Spirit will teach you in that very hour what you ought to say.* I realize that this is referring to when we are being persecuted and questioned, but this same principle can be applied to our teaching. Yes, we study to show ourselves approved (2 Tim. 2:15), but we need to also learn to allow the Holy Spirit to enable us to teach by taking that knowledge and speaking through our mouths as He gives it to us. One reference is in Acts 8:35 which says: *Then Philip **opened his mouth**, and beginning at this Scripture, preached Jesus to him.* Another one from Acts 10:34 says, *Then Peter **opened his***

mouth *and said: "In truth I perceive that God shows no partiality".* Of course they opened their mouths! Why does it say that? Because they opened their mouths and the Holy Spirit took over. It was the gift of teaching. It operates the same way with preaching because it is the Spirit of God referred to throughout the Old and New Testaments. God uses us as the vessel and we speak his oracles or message. That does not mean that you have to do it as an impromptu speech, it just means that you have to let God speak through you. Have you ever thought that one speaker sounded "anointed" and another does not? That is because the Holy Spirit is aiding some in preaching and others are relying mostly on their own intellect. God uses everyday people like Peter and Philip to preach and teach his Word.

The Nicolaitan doctrine would have us believe that we are made able to preach and teach the Word of God by a seminary education.

Most of these classes are taught with the intellectual ability only. The majority of these professors are very intelligent and have earned doctor's degrees the hard way with a lot of work invested. That is why many of the students do not question them. They have established a position of authority to a point where people are afraid to argue or disagree because they will be made to look like a fool or they will fail the class. I have learned under some of those teachers who were anointed by God. I have studied under some who obviously only did it as a vocation and had missed their calling to do something else. The most dangerous group was those who started out with a calling from God, but fell into the trap of the Nicolaitan spirit or their own ego and strayed away from belief in God's Word. They would teach classes that were very interesting and seemed to be inspired by the Holy Spirit, but they, in fact, were inspired by some other spirit. The fruit of that class turned out to be unbelief rather than faith.

God calls and enables his teachers and preachers with the empowerment of the Holy Spirit. We are called by his Spirit and affirmed and trained by others with the same callings who have been given much wisdom, discernment, and spiritual maturity. Again, that enables us to function in direct connection to God with the empowerment of his Spirit and bestowment of his gifts from Him.

OTHER MINISTRY GIFTS

1 Corinthians 12:27 says:

"Now you are the body of Christ, and members individually. [28] *And God has appointed these in the church: first apostles, second prophets, third teachers, after that miracles, then gifts of healings, helps, administrations, varieties of tongues.*

Miracles, healings, and varieties of tongues sound more like the "manifestation gifts" mentioned earlier in the chapter. These are gifts that were bestowed as needed at the particular moment by an instantaneous endowment of the Holy Spirit. However, these particular three were also mentioned with the same ministry gifts mentioned in Ephesians 5. There are some set in the Body of Christ who have the particular function of praying for and receiving miracles and others who have healing faith. There are others who seem to be regular deliverers of messages of tongues and interpretation of those tongues. These are definitely ministries that cannot be taught, but can only come from an intense and close relationship to God.

The other gifts mentioned, helps and administrations, are vitally important ministries that keep the church functioning and producing fruit. "Administrations" is almost always looked at as a function that someone that has to be taught. However, we all know that many people who wind up administrating have no business being there no matter how much training they have had. I look at it like those who want to be the "boss" the most, usually have no business being there. They turn out to be control freaks and micro-managers. They have no compassion on other people around them and look only to inward self-satisfaction as the ultimate goal of what is being accomplished. The one thing missing is what Jesus said must be there for a leader; *humility* (*...the last shall be first*).

A true leader is recognized by the sheep. They have love, humility, and they would rather not be leading, but rather following and helping. Since they do not have a desire to "bulldoze" their way to the top, they often do not wind up there. Jesus said,

"My **sheep** hear My voice, and I know them, and they **follow** Me." (John 10:27). When someone has been handed a leadership job by the Chief Shepherd, he is letting Jesus work through him and the sheep recognize Jesus in him or her. That person has the gift of organization and orderliness. They are disciplined and sensitive to both the people and the Spirit of God. The Church cannot function without them. It is a vital ministry that God has appointed.

The other ministry mentioned called **helps** can cover a multitude of areas. The Holy Spirit himself is called "the Helper". A helper in the Body of Christ can help someone with physical tasks or with things that are spiritual. They want to help people. They have the heart of a servant and love to serve. It might be setting up for an outreach ministry, going on a mission trip, working with a food ministry or building a wheelchair ramp. Some are always ready to prepare food or make things for those who are having a hard time. I believe that more people have been brought to Christ through the ministry of helps than the ministry of the evangelist. The truth is, they work hand-in-hand. The Gospel is delivered to people who are drawn to it. Many times those people's attention have been grabbed after their needs were met. Those needs were met by those with the gift of helps. The gift of helps often reaches into the spiritual realm by those who help others by intercessory prayer or helping them have the faith to get through a situation that has them burdened down. You can even help someone recognize gifts and ministries that God has given them. One of the greatest helps is the gift of encouragement. God uses people to encourage others and help them realize that they are a valuable asset to the Kingdom.

There are other ministry gifts mentioned in Romans 12. There are even others that are obvious that are not mentioned in the Bible at all. Those to do with worship, music, creativity, writing, etc. The list could branch out and reach into the hundreds or thousands. Think what could happen if God's people started using all of those gifts rather than depending on one person to do all of the work of Christ! It is happening right now all over the world, but it is also being stifled in too many places. Do you see why Jesus hates the doctrine of the Nicolaitans? He hates it for our sake, not His.

Chapter 10

WARNING TO THE NICOLAITANS

As I said earlier in this book, the Nicolaitans of Jesus time of ministry on this earth were the Jewish religious leaders. I believe that these same warnings apply to past, present, and future. The way Jesus describes those who adhere to this doctrine is as follows from Matthew 23:

Woe to the Scribes and Pharisees

1 Then Jesus spoke to the multitudes and to His disciples, 2 saying: "The scribes and the Pharisees sit in Moses' seat. 3 Therefore whatever they tell you to observe, that observe and do, but do not do according to their works; **for they say, and do not do**. *⁴ For they* bind heavy burdens, hard to bear, and lay them on men's shoulders; but they themselves will not move them with one of their fingers. *⁵ **But all their works they do to be seen by men**. They make their phylacteries broad and enlarge the borders of their garments. *⁶ They love the best places at feasts, the best seats in the synagogues, ⁷ greetings in the marketplaces, and to be called by men, 'Rabbi, Rabbi.' ⁸ **But you, do not be called 'Rabbi'; for One is your Teacher, the Christ, and you are all brethren. ⁹ Do not call anyone on earth your father; for One is your Father, He who is in heaven. ¹⁰ And do not be called teachers; for One is your Teacher, the Christ. ¹¹ But he who is greatest among you shall be your servant. ¹² And whoever exalts himself will be humbled, and he who humbles himself will be exalted.**

[13] *"But woe to you, scribes and Pharisees, hypocrites! For you shut up the kingdom of heaven against men; for you neither go in yourselves, nor do you allow those who are entering to go in.* [14] *Woe to you, scribes and Pharisees, hypocrites! For you devour widows' houses, and for a pretense make long prayers. Therefore, you will receive greater condemnation.*

[15] *"Woe to you, scribes and Pharisees, hypocrites! For you travel land and sea to win one proselyte, and when he is won, you make him twice as much a son of hell as yourselves.*

[16] *"Woe to you, blind guides, who say, 'Whoever swears by the temple, it is nothing; but whoever swears by the gold of the temple, he is obliged to perform it.'* [17] *Fools and blind! For which is greater, the gold or the temple that sanctifies[d] the gold?* [18] *And, 'Whoever swears by the altar, it is nothing; but whoever swears by the gift that is on it, he is obliged to perform it.'* [19] *Fools and blind! For which is greater,*

the gift or the altar that sanctifies the gift? [20] Therefore he who swears by the altar, swears by it and by all things on it. [21] He who swears by the temple, swears by it and by Him who dwells in it. [22] And he who swears by heaven, swears by the throne of God and by Him who sits on it.

[23] "Woe to you, scribes and Pharisees, hypocrites! For you pay tithe of mint and anise and cumin, and have neglected the weightier matters of the law: justice and mercy and faith. These you ought to have done, without leaving the others undone. [24] Blind guides, who strain out a gnat and swallow a camel!

[25] "Woe to you, scribes and Pharisees, hypocrites! For you cleanse the outside of the cup and dish, but **inside they are full of extortion and self-indulgence.** [26] Blind Pharisee, first cleanse the inside of the cup and dish, that the outside of them may be clean also.

[27] "Woe to you, scribes and Pharisees, hypocrites! For you are like whitewashed tombs

*which indeed appear beautiful outwardly, but inside are full of dead men's bones and all uncleanness. ²⁸ Even so you also outwardly appear righteous to men, **but inside you are full of hypocrisy and lawlessness.***

²⁹ *"Woe to you, scribes and Pharisees, hypocrites! Because you build the tombs of the prophets and adorn the monuments of the righteous, ³⁰ and say, 'If we had lived in the days of our fathers, we would not have been partakers with them in the blood of the prophets.'*

³¹ *"Therefore you are witnesses against yourselves that you are sons of those who murdered the prophets. ³² Fill up, then, the measure of your fathers' guilt. ³³ Serpents, brood of vipers! How can you escape the condemnation of hell?*

Not my words; His. Surely that doesn't apply to us today! That's what the Pharisees said then too. Satan started out as an angel of God. His thoughts turned inward and away from glorifying God. Isaiah 14 says:

12"How you are fallen from heaven,

O Lucifer, son of the morning!

How you are cut down to the ground,

You who weakened the nations!

13 For you have said in your heart:

'I will ascend into heaven,

I will exalt my throne above the stars of God;

I will also sit on the mount of the congregation

On the farthest sides of the north;

14 I will ascend above the heights of the clouds,

I will be like the Most High.'

15 Yet you shall be brought down to Sheol,

To the lowest depths of the Pit.

The sin of pride is Satan's favorite sin because it is his character. Taking our eyes off of Jesus and upon ourselves is the temptation that caused the fall of mankind. Adam and Eve first looked at the serpent who caused them to look at him and take their eyes off of the Lord. Then they looked at the forbidden fruit, then began to doubt God's word, then he had them looking at themselves and imagining how they could be equal with God. This same temptation happens with God's called messengers in many forms. We can be tempted to be or do something more than God intended for us. We can be enticed to bring glory to ourselves or take credit for something that God should be given credit for doing. Many times, I see pastors who do not believe God's Word anymore who used to believe it. They act as if they were "enlightened", but in most cases thus far, I have found that they were involved in some sin that they didn't want to give up and the only way they could cope with the guilt was to quit believing the Bible. The same tactic Satan used on Adam and Eve to get them to eat the forbidden fruit. Once these temptations are succumbed to, the enemy has a vessel who will bring false teaching to the Church and will be believed by some of them because he or she has that power or authority ascribed to them by the Nicolaitan belief.

There are many pastors and ministers who are whole-heartedly serving God and bearing fruit today. They are simply doing it God's way. God is calling us all to go along with His plan to do the same thing. To those who are not, He already gave simple instructions as how to fix the problem. He said in Revelation 2 to "**repent**". That's right, confess it as sin, ask forgiveness and turn the other way and start walking in humility with the Lord and seeking his will for your life. Those who are following Him always need to be on guard for temptation or deception so we will also stay on his course. Here are some guidelines to keep us from falling: (**Jude 24-25** *Now to Him who is able to keep you from stumbling, And to present you faultless Before the presence of His glory with exceeding joy, To God our Savior, Who alone is wise, Be glory* *and majesty, Dominion and power, Both now and forever. Amen.)*

Guidelines to keep us from falling:

1. **Make prayer, and lots of it, a priority.** (More than the national average for pastors which is about 3 minutes a day.)
2. **Check your heart.** What are my motives for doing what I'm doing?
3. **Examine yourself daily.** If I see a sin, whether it is obvious or not, call it a sin and repent of it. If you do it again, do the same thing until it is gone.
4. Continue to **grow in that close and intimate relationship with Jesus.** (If you don't know what I'm talking about, go back to square one and pray to be born-again as Jesus said in John 3:3.)
5. **Be filled with the Spirit.** You need to receive that initial empowerment

as described in Acts 2, 8, 10, 19 and throughout the book. Then pray to continue to be filled daily (Ephesians 5:18). Stay filled through worship, prayer, and serving God.

6. **James 4:10** *Humble yourselves* in the sight of the Lord, and He will lift you up. Do not worry about exalting yourself. He will do that for you. He will also keep you from being too full of yourself so you won't trip over yourself and fall flat on your face.

7. **Walk in the Spirit** and you will not fulfill the lusts of the flesh (Galatians 5:16). The way to avoid sin and temptation is not to fight it, but to walk with Jesus. The rest of Galatians 5 is well-known for telling us the difference between walking in the Spirit and the flesh. I believe another version is in 2 Peter 1 which says: *5 But also for this very reason, giving all diligence, add*

*to your faith virtue, to virtue knowledge,
⁶ to knowledge self-control, to self-control perseverance, to perseverance godliness, ⁷ to godliness brotherly kindness, and to brotherly kindness love. ⁸ For if these things are yours and abound, you will be neither barren nor unfruitful in the knowledge of our Lord Jesus Christ. ⁹ For he who lacks these things is shortsighted, even to blindness, and has forgotten that he was cleansed from his old sins.*

¹⁰ Therefore, brethren, be even more diligent to make your call and election sure, for if you do these things you will never stumble; **¹¹** for **so an entrance** *will be supplied to you abundantly into the everlasting kingdom of our Lord and Savior Jesus Christ.*

Look at verse 10! It says if we do these things, we will make our calling and election sure and never stumble! The way to avoid falling into the trap of a Nicolaitan is to walk close to the Father by walking in the Spirit. Also, look at the phrase, "so an entrance will be supplied to you...". Remember when Jesus told Peter "I will give you the keys to the Kingdom..." in Matthew 16:19? He was not making Peter the gate keeper like we always see illustrated in the jokes. Peter just told us what those keys were in this chapter: Faith, virtue, knowledge, self-control, perseverance, godliness, brotherly kindness (phileo), and love (agape). Paul called it the fruit of the Spirit, Peter called it the "entrance" or the keys to the Kingdom. Not only does it allow us into the Kingdom of God, but it allows the Kingdom of God into us in the here-and-now. That is the secret to "not stumbling". Walk with Jesus in the Spirit.

CONCLUSION

WORD TO THE CHURCH

1 Timothy 2:5

For there is one God and **one Mediator** *between God and men, the Man Christ Jesus.*

The word of the Messiah to his people is "I LOVE YOU"! He wants us to receive that love to its fullest and for us to give it back without any interference or filters. Jesus hates the doctrines and deeds of the Nicolaitans because they interfere with that reciprocation of love.

We do not need someone to slow down that exchange of love between us and the Savior by redirecting it in any way. Our relationship with God needs to be one-on-one where He can develop us into the persons he created us to be. He can infuse our unique personalities with his Spirit and make us into that person that we were originally created to be.

I catch myself wanting to insert disclaimers throughout this book, but I keep hearing from the Holy Spirit, "do not hold back; do not compromise". Jesus did not try to be politically correct or diplomatic when He addressed the Pharisees or in Revelation 2 and 3 where He admonished and rebuked the seven churches. I do not expect everyone to accept this with open arms. I fully expect to be ostracized by many of my peers and to receive an onslaught of theological explanations as to why I am wrong. I might even be called a heretic (thank God it is not legal to burn someone at the stake today).

All I know is, this message was put on my heart over forty years ago and it has grown stronger no matter how I have tried to pass it off or ignore it. That is why I am basing all of this on Scripture and not on what man has inserted along the way to make it mean something else. I have to answer to God and God alone for what I did with this message, which brings us back to the message itself, **it all comes down to our personal relationship with God.** When we stand before Him at the judgement seat, we cannot blame anything on any other man, priest, mediator. Our only defense will be that what we did in our own lives will be made right through the only Mediator that counts; Jesus Christ.

WHAT DO WE DO NOW?

I cannot speak for you and your personal situation. If I did that, I would be a Nicolaitan, wouldn't I? You will need to personally seek the guidance of the Holy Spirit and confirm it with Scripture and even confirm it again in whatever way God wants to show you. I am not calling for a mass pulling-out of all denominations. If the Nicolaitan spirit is still there, it will only find a new way to manifest.

We need a mass repentance. Jesus' answer to all the churches in Asia that He admonished was to **repent**. That would involve confessing that we relied upon others to do what God had called us to do, asking Him to give us the ability and strength do turn from that, and asking the Holy Spirit to show us what to do next. Recognize the gifts that God has given you and start using them. Quit making excuses and just go out and serve the Lord with all your heart. Dive deep into your relationship with Him and **know Him** intimately as you have never known Him before. Become familiar with the voice of the Holy Spirit and God's guidance where you recognize the Shepherd whenever He speaks.

Do not tell your pastor that he is a heretic and out of the will of God. God may already have dealt with him long before you. This is a personal thing, so grow in that relationship with Jesus and begin serving Him with all of your heart. I guarantee, when your pastor sees that happen, he will notice! I notice when someone from the church, where I am pastor, has realized that God has a plan and purpose for their life. This will immediately increase the ministry power of the Church. When more people begin to recognize their own gifts and talents and use them, each part of the Body of Christ will fit into place and will begin to function as it was meant to be. The pastor will be more effective because he is doing what God intended also. All of the ministry gifts will begin to function and there will be a great revival that will affect the whole world.

A wonderful example of this is found in Acts chapter 6. It went like this:

"Now in those days, when the number of the disciples was multiplying, there arose a complaint against the Hebrews by the Hellenists, because their widows were neglected in the daily distribution. ² Then the twelve summoned the multitude of the disciples and said, "It is not desirable that we should leave the word of God and serve tables. ³ Therefore, brethren, seek out from among you seven men of good reputation, full of the Holy Spirit and wisdom, whom we may appoint over this business; ⁴ but we will give ourselves continually to prayer and to the ministry of the word."

⁵ And the saying pleased the whole multitude. And they chose Stephen, a man full of faith and the Holy Spirit, and Philip, Prochorus, Nicanor, Timon, Parmenas, and Nicolas, a proselyte from Antioch, ⁶ whom they set before the apostles; and when they had prayed, they laid hands on them.

⁷ Then the word of God spread, and the number of the disciples multiplied greatly in Jerusalem, and a great many of the priests were obedient to the faith.

Look at verse 7!

1. The Word of God spread.

2. The number of disciples multiplied.

3. Even the priests were obedient to the faith!

We do not try to start a movement; we simply allow the movement of the Holy Spirit in our lives. The Lord will take care of the rest if we do what we are called to do. We do not try to make anyone else change; we allow Him to change us. In Acts 6, the need arose, the Spirit moved, more people found their calling. The roles of these deacons were not any less important nor had any less impact than the apostles who were praying and seeking God. Their requirements were *wisdom, being of good reputation, full of faith, and* **full of the Holy Spirit.** Stephen became the first martyr to be stoned to death for preaching the Gospel. Stephen is the one who saw Jesus standing, not sitting, by the right hand of the Father when he was about to go home. Philip was the first to get the Gospel to the Ethiopians by preaching to the eunuch and baptizing him, then Philip was transported to another place by the Spirit. These men did not get assigned to this ministry of a deacon because they were "less spiritual." Their ministries actually increased and blossomed because they found their niche' in the Body of Christ. That is exactly what will happen to us when we act upon that calling that God has given us.

What is that calling that God has given us? I've already said that we are ministers of reconciliation; reconciling people to God. But what is my individual calling? Don't ask me, don't ask your minister, don't ask your best friend, or spouse, or counselor; ask God! Yes, He wants you to just step onto the water and walk. He wants you to ask Him directly. He might show you through different means or methods. It might take a while, or He might show you immediately. He **will** show you though; that is guaranteed. James 1:5 -*If any of you lacks wisdom, let him ask of God, who gives to all liberally and without reproach, and it will be given to him.*

Why did Jesus use such strong words as "hate" when He addressed the deeds and doctrines of the Nicolaitans? Because He loves us so much. Romans 8:38 and 39 says:

__38__ For I am persuaded that neither death nor life, nor angels nor principalities nor powers, nor things present nor things to come, __39__ nor height nor depth, nor any other created thing, shall be able to separate us from the love of God which is in Christ Jesus our Lord.

Nor Nicolaitans… Ask Him directly and see what He says.

CPSIA information can be obtained
at www.ICGtesting.com
Printed in the USA
LVOW04s0407260716
497727LV00007B/25/P